Ex Libris

Marjorie K. Sampson

NORTH IN THE WORLD

≈ ≈ ≈ ≈ ≈

NORTH IN THE WORLD

SELECTED POEMS OF ROLF JACOBSEN

A Bilingual Edition

Translated, edited, and introduced by
Roger Greenwald

The University of Chicago Press
Chicago and London

ROLF JACOBSEN (1907–1994) published twelve books of poetry and six collections; his work has been translated into more than twenty languages. He was a member of the Norwegian Academy of Language and Literature and was awarded the Norwegian Critics' Prize (1960), the Aschehoug Prize (1986), the Dobloug Prize (1968), and the Grand Nordic Prize (1989).

ROGER GREENWALD is the author of one book of poems, *Connecting Flight,* and the translator of several works from Scandinavian languages, including *The Silence Afterwards: Selected Poems of Rolf Jacobsen; Through Naked Branches: Selected Poems of Tarjei Vesaas;* and *A Story about Mr. Silberstein,* by Erland Josephson. He is the recipient of the CBC Radio/*Saturday Night* Literary Award for poetry, as well as of numerous translation prizes.

Frontispiece: Rolf Jacobsen, summer 1956 (photograph courtesy Gyldendal Norsk Forlag)

The University of Chicago Press, Chicago 60637
The University of Chicago Press, Ltd., London
Norwegian poems © 1999 by Gyldendal Norsk Forlag ASA
English translations © 1985, 1997, 2002 by Roger Greenwald
Introduction and notes © 1985, 2002 by Roger Greenwald
All rights reserved. Published 2002
Printed in the United States of America

11 10 09 08 07 06 05 04 03 02   1 2 3 4 5

ISBN: 0-226-39035-7 (cloth)

The University of Chicago Press gratefully acknowledges the support of Institusjonen Fritt Ord, Oslo, toward the publication of this book.

Library of Congress Cataloging-in-Publication Data

Jacobsen, Rolf.
    North in the world : selected poems of Rolf Jacobsen / a bilingual edition translated, edited, and introduced by Roger Greenwald.
        p. cm.
    Includes bibliographical references and indexes.
    ISBN 0-226-39035-7 (cloth : alk. paper)
        I. Greenwald, Roger, date. II. Title.

PT8951.2.A38 N33 2002
839.9'2172—dc21

                                                    2001050182

⊗The paper used in this publication meets the minimum requirements of the American National Standard for Information Sciences—Permanence of Paper for Printed Library Materials, ANSI Z39.48–1992.

These translations are dedicated to
Luigi M. Bianchi
in gratitude for enduring friendship

Contents

Acknowledgments

A great many people have helped me in various ways in my work with Jacobsen's poems over the past twenty years. The foremost was Rolf Jacobsen himself, who was generous and patient in answering my many questions. Of the half dozen people who have read and commented on whole drafts or selected translations, Richard M. Lush and Inger Haug stand out for having stayed the course throughout my engagement with this work. Paal-Helge Haugen, in addition to having commented on the original version of the introduction, has remained "on call" for urgent questions about nuances of the Norwegian. Eva Lie-Nielsen at Gyldendal Norsk Forlag has been a friend and support through many ups and downs. And for the present edition I owe special debts of gratitude to Hanne Lillebo, who has shared her expertise on textual and biographical matters; to Lasse Tømte, who has gone over all the translations against the originals and offered me detailed comments; and to Frankie Shackelford, who has given me the benefit of her keen ear for both Norwegian and English.

I am grateful also to the publishers and editors who saw fit to publish the earlier selections of Rolf Jacobsen's poetry that I translated and edited. Ninety-six of the 121 translations in this book, as well as the introduction and most of the endnotes, appeared in *The Silence Afterwards: Selected Poems of Rolf Jacobsen* (Princeton University Press, 1985). I have revised many of these translations for this edition; and I have revised and supplemented the front and back matter. Twenty-one of the translations in this book appeared in Rolf Jacobsen, *Did I Know You?* (Gyldendal Norsk Forlag, 1997); I have revised some of these for this edition. Four translations appear for the first time in this book.

I thank Norwegian Literature Abroad for covering some of the costs of translation. Ian McInnis and Shahir al Rashid generously provided technical assistance in preparing scans of Kjell Varvin's artwork for the jacket, and Gyldendal Norsk Forlag provided scans of the four photos of Rolf Jacobsen.

Roger Greenwald

Introduction

Rolf Jacobsen's Poetry

Rolf Jacobsen's poetry is special for two reasons: because it opened a new chapter in Norwegian poetry, and because it explores life with a distinctive sensibility and voice.

Rolf Jacobsen was born on 8 March 1907 and died on 20 February 1994. He spent the first part of his childhood in Oslo, and studied there from his teen years into his late twenties. But from the age of six to thirteen he lived with his family in several villages in the countryside along the River Glomma, an area to which he returned when he was twenty-seven. He eventually settled in the town of Hamar, a regional center about sixty miles (ninety-five kilometers) north of Oslo, on the eastern shore of Lake Mjøsa. He made his living as a journalist and newspaper editor.[1]

In 1933, when Jacobsen published his first book, most poetry in Norway was still written in traditional meters, and most of it was rhymed. It drew its images from traditional sources—myth, nature, religion, seafaring, and warfare—and almost always, it maintained an elevated, "poetic" tone.

Jacobsen's first book broke new ground: many of the poems were in unrhymed free verse, and used diction and vocabulary close to those of speech; and many treated subjects or used images drawn from the modern industrial city. Of course Jacobsen had some forerunners in Norway. Several poets of stature departed from standard meters on occasion, and the proletarian writer Kristofer Uppdal (1878–1961) made use of unvarnished details from urban and industrial life. But Jacobsen is now widely regarded as the poet who launched modernism in his country (the poet Claes Gill [1910–1973] made an important contribution a few years later). It is not necessary to conduct a detailed analysis to convince oneself how far Jacobsen had come. Notwithstanding the connecting threads that can always be traced from one period to the next, anyone who reads aloud a few lyrics by Bjørnstjerne Bjørnson (1832–1910) and a few by Jacobsen will hear the nineteenth century in one ear and the twentieth in the other.[2]

---

1. Readers who would like more biographical information about Jacobsen are referred to *World Authors 1985–1990*, ed. Vineta Colby (New York: Wilson, 1995).

2. An examination of the ways in which Jacobsen's choice of words enriched and renewed poetic vocabulary in Norwegian lies beyond the scope of this introduction and also beyond my area of competence.

The change to what we now regard as modern subjects and styles was slow in coming to Norway. The new era had already arrived in the poetry of several other countries. But Jacobsen's poems in the modern style are not mere imitations of imported models; poems like "Reise" ("Travel") and "Byens metafysikk" ("Metaphysics of the City") show that he had made a new way of looking and writing his own.

Yet in *Jord og jern* (Earth and Iron), as the title suggests, Jacobsen took care to forge a connection between the old and the new. The titles in the book's first section indicate subjects drawn from nature; almost all of these poems are in unrhymed free verse. It is as if Jacobsen drew his readers into the new style with themes he knew they would be comfortable with. The poems in the third section bring us unambiguously into the modern world; yet here Jacobsen does not hesitate, in treating urban themes, to use rhyme or fairly regular meter occasionally when they suit his purposes.

Because Jacobsen seemed at first to be a champion of technological progress, member of a generation that could find poetry in machines, much has been written about his supposed later change from an admirer to a skeptic or outright critic of technology. But even in his first two books he distinguishes between beneficial and oppressive aspects of the modern scene, and often finds each aspect implicit in the other. In "Dirrende telefonstolper" ("Vibrating Telephone Poles"), for example, the message is mixed: the poles as antennas listening to outer space are at first presented as wonderful; the signals they pick up are described, by the end of the poem, with horrifying images. In treating technologies, Jacobsen always focuses on the relation they have, as phenomena or as metaphors, to what he considers compatible with human nature. That is why air travel, subways, television, and advertising earn harsh treatment, newspapers and radio get better than even breaks, and railroads inspire lifelong admiration.

It will repay the reader to trace the railroad as it winds its way through Jacobsen's books. On the historical plane (which became steadily more important in relation to many subjects as Jacobsen's work matured), the English-speaking reader needs to know that the building of Norway's railroads in the second half of the nineteenth century and the beginning of the twentieth not only bound together some of the distant and isolated parts of a country that extends for over a thousand miles (seventeen hundred kilometers), but represented a feat of railway engineering unrivaled anywhere. The *rallare* (navvies) who built the railroads still have, for

Rolf Jacobsen as a debutant, circa 1933
(photograph courtesy Gyldendal Norsk Forlag)

many Norwegians, the status of folk heroes. Moreover, the Norwegian railroad, as a state-owned enterprise, can be felt by ordinary Norwegian citizens to be in some sense "theirs."

The subject seems inexhaustible for Jacobsen, and his meditations on it increased in complexity. "Jernbaneland" ("Railroad Country"), in his first book, suggests how rich the subject is for the poet at the beginning of his career. The poem's last section, a sort of industrial "call of the wild" that bears a strong flavor of the 1930s, has obvious sexual undertones, and makes plain the speaker's ambivalence about what is freedom, what escapism. Eleven books later, in "Inlandsbanan" ("The Inland Line"), we find the poet riding past abandoned towns on a decaying Swedish line built long ago, at high human cost, to transport soldiers and their weapons. As if that weren't bad enough, at the end of the poem the whole bewildering modern world intrudes by way of newspapers brought aboard for sale. Yet even here, amid the sorrow, we pick up in the evoked journey a whiff of something more than nostalgia: the ineradicable scent of travel. For Jacobsen rode the trains, lived near them, watched them and listened to them, and wrote some of his best poems about them. And the Norwegian State Railway returned the favor by giving the poet a pass for a free trip each year!

~

Jacobsen's poetry is, of course, much more than a penetrating commentary on the modern external world, and indeed, this aspect of his work becomes less important, though no less evident, as soon as one turns to his third and fourth books, *Fjerntog* (Express Train) and *Hemmelig liv* (Secret Life). Here the poems seem to come from a greater depth: they emerge from contemplation (not without humor); they deal with eternal themes as well as with the current condition; and they begin to show a conscious use of history. Poems such as "Solsikke" ("Sunflower"), "På Varaldskogen" ("In the Varald Forest"), "Tømmer" ("Timber"), "Alderdommen" ("Old Age"), "Turnipshøst" ("Turnip Crop"), "Sorgfulle tårn" ("Mournful Towers"), and "Stavkirker" ("Stave Churches") force us to consider what is fundamental to the way Jacobsen wrote for the rest of his life.

Jacobsen's writing combines an ancient way of looking—a way that searches for connectedness—with an openness to the new, even to things that reveal no connectedness and would resist attempts to impose it. In other words, Jacobsen has a strong sense of the world as mystery, and he approaches that mystery with reverence. His sensibility is a religious one—not much concerned with doctrine but very much concerned with spirit, with the preciousness of life, with unity, and with the exertions necessary to receive ever fresh manifestations of these qualities.[3] It is not important whether one takes "receive" literally or as a metaphor for a certain type of experience. What is important is that even in his less suc-

---

3. Jacobsen converted to Roman Catholicism in 1951. The influence of his faith on his later poetry is a topic this introduction does not address, but the reader will note certain connections, perhaps most readily in Jacobsen's interest in the medieval monasteries.

cessful poems, Jacobsen can never be accused of opportunism toward his subjects. His world is not fodder for technique. It may be that Jacobsen receives certain types of meaning more readily and more clearly than others, but that does not mean he tries to subsume the whole world in one Procrustean song. His sensibility is receptive and contemplative, yet does not need to deny or divest itself of personality in the Western sense. All that is required is a measure of humility.

The way Jacobsen writes evinces humility at every turn. In the first place, he tries to create poems that are accessible but not oversimplified. Second, he concentrates on subjects other than the self, treating himself mainly as an instrument for their elucidation. Where the voice is powerful and heavily stressed, as in "Sorgfulle tårn" ("Mournful Towers") or "Stenhistorien" ("The History of Stone"), the forcefulness comes to inhere in the subject; it does not insist on itself as a quality of the speaker's. Even the poems that refer to themselves often declare that the natural world acts upon them, rather than the other way around. In "Grønt lys" ("Green Light"), for example, the poet says that the winds spread his poem out like dust and that seeds sprout between the letters in his words.

Jacobsen scarcely puts himself forward at all. We learn only a little about his everyday life from his poems, and almost nothing about his personal relations. He is concerned to render his experience of his own and his readers' surroundings, and the ideas and feelings that attach to that encounter. His poems do not pay much attention to the occupations of his body or the workings of his unconscious. They are more closely aligned to the seasons of the earth than to the inclinations of the ego.

The importance of nature in Jacobsen's work is obvious, and places him in a long tradition of Norwegian writing. The rivers, mountains, trees, stones, and skies of Norway serve as settings, as characters, and as sources of metaphor. Jacobsen is interested in people's relation to the natural world, their relation to the man-made world, and the ways in which these two relations affect each other. His sensitivity to nature, and the access to self that it grants him, inform both his enthusiasms and his regrets about our culture.

English-speaking readers need to keep a few things in mind if they are to grasp this dimension of Jacobsen's poetry. First, we sometimes need to ask ourselves what is happening. Poems such as "Nu bærer elven sine lamper ut" ("Now the River Is Carrying Off Its Lights") or "Fossestøperen" ("The Foundryman of Waterfalls"), for example, will make immediate sense to Norwegian readers, but may seem mysterious to us unless we realize, in one case, that the time is summer and the streams are drying up, and in the other, that waterfalls in forests make certain kinds of sound.

Second, we need to realize that although the ways in which Jacobsen treats nature can be analyzed and his attitudes toward it studied in relation to those of various literary traditions, it would be a mistake to regard the pervasiveness of nature in his work as the product mainly of one or another literary stance. Nature is a powerful presence in Norway, and few Norwegians of Jacobsen's century grew up without a strong sense of that presence. Jacobsen, like any Norwegian poet who decides to speak of nature at all, is dealing with an everyday fact of life, a form and a force with which he is on intimate terms.

A mountain has one kind of effect on people who are looking at it as tourists, with urban shapes and scales in their heads, and another kind of effect on people who have walked its paths and climbed its rocks year in and year out. Once again, we see that Jacobsen's surroundings are not "material" for poems, but almost internalized parts of the speaker. The result is an unusual quality—perhaps shared by some Chinese and Japanese writing: the poet does not enter the rock; the rock has entered the poet, and the poet takes account of that when he speaks.

~

What, then, is the method that Jacobsen developed to embody his mode of seeing and listening? Taking his cue from a poem in *Headlines*, the Danish poet and critic Poul Borum writes that Jacobsen attempts,

> through imaginative perception, to create a balance between metaphor and myth, that is, between transformation and unity. His fundamental experience of the world (people, nature, culture) is transforming, is a paraphrasing in images, a saying that this is like something else, but the core is tremblingly static, is myth. That this myth is empty is a basic condition in modernism and in the twentieth century. The emptiness, seen negatively, is the stagnation in the midst of transformation—Rolf Jacobsen's fear of the transitional states of morning and evening; experienced positively, it is stillness, the innermost mystic silence— his cultivation of the unity day-and-night. Anxiety is mastered with the imagination's precision, and the eternal is discovered in the eternally fleeting.[4]

4. Borum, "Rolf Jacobsens hemmelige sprog," *Minervas Kvartalskrift*, I (1970), 37 (my translation).

Silence lies at the core of Jacobsen's work in more senses than one. That he often takes it as his subject is obvious from titles like "Tausheten i trær" ("The Silence in Trees") and "Stillheten efterpå" ("The Silence Afterwards"). Jacobsen's use of images, by powerfully evoking the visual and often by setting two pictures side by side, moves the reader beyond words and into a "silent" realm. Despite marked differences in style, one could say that Jacobsen's work anticipates a quality that Ted Hughes noted among poets of Eastern Europe in the next generation (Vasko Popa, Miroslav Holub, Zbigniew Herbert): that they aim at "making audible meaning without disturbing the silence."[5] Certainly Jacobsen is a poet with a profound respect both for the silence that precedes and follows his acts of speech and for the silence that inheres in things: their unnamable qualities, which the writer must respect if his efforts are to yield up some sense of them.

Jacobsen's practice of presenting not only plants and animals but inanimate objects as if they were endowed with human capacities of observation and feeling reflects his effort to discover unspoken truths about his surroundings and about us. Seen from outside, this practice can be called simply "personification"; and indeed, when the poems fail, the method can seem to be little more than a device. But when the poems succeed, they capture a strange and delicate quality, and sometimes give us the eerie sensation that we are being regarded; so it is clear that Jacobsen has arrived at the heart of his subject. Such success cannot be the result of the mechanical application of a device. An observation by Walter Benjamin provides a useful way of thinking about the process and the impulse that lies behind it: "To perceive the aura of an object, we look at means to invest it with the ability to look at us in return."[6]

In Poul Borum's elegant description,

> [Jacobsen's] double task has been to give his lightness weight and his gravity lightness—where the first fails, the poems flutter off without obligations, like paper butterflies of metaphor, and where the second fails, they sink to the ground like unambiguous (satiric or tragic) fragments of myth. The most successful poems in his books could be called *metaphor-myths;* they attain effort-

5. "Introduction," in Vasko Popa, *Collected Poems,* trans. Anne Pennington (New York: Persea, 1978), 3.

6. Benjamin, "On Some Motifs in Baudelaire," in *Illuminations,* trans. Harry Zohn (New York: Harcourt, Brace & World, 1968), 188.

lessly the nervous partnership of unity and transformation that
is his fundamental experience.[7]

Especially in poems that capture the spirit of place, we can see Jacob-
sen's search for unity and his respect for silence as two aspects of the same
posture. "Avaldsnes," "Bortafor Grorud—" ("Beyond Grorud—"),
"Tårnene i Bologna" ("The Towers in Bologna"), "Avignon, Vaucluse,"
"Små byer i Auvergne" ("Old Cities in Auvergne"), "Klokkene fra As-
sisi" ("The Bells from Assisi"), "'Silvery Moon'"—all these poems evoke
not only the particular flavor of the places contemplated, but a hovering
presence that gives each place a niche in a larger expanse, just as the place
seems to set the human observer (and the reader) in one of its inconspic-
uous corners, like a tiny figure in a Chinese landscape painting.

~

If we look closely at Jacobsen's poems with a view to understanding how
their verbal textures embody his attitudes toward both language and the
world, we will notice a quality that the American critic and translator
James Larson has aptly called decorum. It is obvious that Jacobsen's choice
of subjects honors, for whatever reason, certain limits drawn around ar-
eas that have often been considered unsuitable for public exposure. But
Larson is making a point not about subject matter, but about words.

> There is one essential quality uniting [Jacobsen's early and later
> works], and it has to do with the unfashionable problem of pro-
> priety or decorum. Jacobsen's ambition as a poet has always been
> to present his subjects naively and distinctly, without addition or
> subtraction. His poetry is clear but not familiar, and simple but
> never facile; its justice lies almost entirely in the choice and pro-
> priety of terms. This is an ambition more praiseworthy than
> brilliant, and it has served—if not in intention, at least in ef-
> fect—to limit his audience and delay recognition.[8]

Larson has pinpointed the principles that govern Jacobsen's poems in-
sofar as they are presentations of subjects (they are also, of course, mu-
sical structures of feeling). Poetry written on these principles is not flashy.
For Jacobsen, things are things and words are words. He introduces ob-
jects into his poems primarily because he wants to say something about
them or wants the reader to see them, not because he wants the sound or

---

7. Borum, 37 (my translation).

8. Larson, review of *Samlede dikt* (1977), *World Literature Today*, 52 (1978), 479.

tone of the words that name them. (Readers who find Jacobsen's use of the definite article as noticeable as I do will perhaps agree that it reflects a deep-seated aspect of his view of his surroundings—a perception of particularity that is childlike, and a conception of archetype that is mythic.) For the most part, Jacobsen is content with the "thingness" of things, and likewise with the "wordness" of words: he does not use words as little visual and sonic objects divorced from meaning. He is masterful in his use of the musical qualities of Norwegian, and from time to time plays with words—breaking them up and getting new meaning out of the pieces, or punning, sometimes across dialects—but the music and the play serve integral purposes in the poems, most often the traditional one of conveying the speaker's attitude toward his subjects and his statements.

It begins to sound as though Jacobsen, the pioneering modernist, is conservative. And in a sense, of course, he is, in that he seeks to conserve certain ancient values in life (contemplation, harmony) and in art (meaning, beauty). But we must go even further and recognize what Larson's description implies: that although Jacobsen broke away from established subjects, treatments, and forms, his method nonetheless has a great deal in common with that of classical authors, in that he aims for simplicity, balance, and controlled, though powerful, emotion. If this is a combination that has deprived Jacobsen's work of allure in a given year's marketplace, it is also a synthesis that has yielded lasting value. The honesty of their engagement with their times has always made the poems seem, on publication, to be current; while their controlled yet unstrained style has kept the best of them—and these are many—from becoming dated. In a large number of Jacobsen's poems, ordinary readers and students of literature alike find that combination of freshness and exact fit of music to both statement and feeling that bestows a permanent "rightness" on a piece of writing. These poems live in the mind, and we go back to them.

~

To read through Jacobsen's collected poems, or even a generous selection, is to become aware of a few long-term developments and many continuing strands. I have already noted some examples of each; here I would like at least to mention a few more—traits that come into sharpest focus when one looks back over a body of work that spans more than fifty years.

Within his framework of metaphor and myth, Poul Borum discerns a development in Jacobsen's work "from the first three books' emphasis on oppositions within similarities to the later books' connection of the large and the small."⁹ Jacobsen's somewhat uncommon interest in effects of scale is certainly evident in many poems from his fourth and later books, for example "Månen og apalen" ("The Moon and the Apple Tree"), "Grønt lys" ("Green Light"), and "Ovenfra, nedenfra og fra siden" ("From Above, from Below and from the Side"). But we can also find such effects, already well developed, in early poems such as "Gummi" ("Rubber") and "Dirrende telefonstolper" ("Vibrating Telephone Poles").

Jacobsen's quest for the spirit of his surroundings often leads him to describe an "other" world behind or beneath the visible one. In reading some of his early poems, such as "Speilglass" ("Plate Glass") or "Den omvendte sommeren" ("The Inverted Summer"), we may wonder whether the poet has detected a truth behind appearances or rather too readily fantasized an alternative existence and sailed off into it. The notion that there is "another" world behind the real one, or through the looking glass, crops up so often that it takes on the flavor of an escapist wish, quite aside from any insights it may offer. It becomes a metaphysical analogue of the longing to travel. But when we arrive at "—En annen sol" ("—A Second Sun"), "Nattvindu" ("Night Window"), and "Tankeløs—" ("Unthinking—"), we see that Jacobsen has firm command of this theme and is using it to get at states of mind that might be inaccessible without it.

On balance, the continuities in Jacobsen's work seem far more striking than the shifts. Strands of recurring but finely adjusted imagery, and of repeated words and phrases, not only contribute to the coherence of his individual volumes but show the constancy of Jacobsen's concerns and his willingness to go back for another try. To take a notable example, Jacobsen has made the image of the earth in space vivid and moving again and again—several times, it is worth remarking, before the Apollo missions brought the picture home on film. Sometimes a phrase in one poem clearly refers to another poem so as to comment or expand on the meaning of the first instance. Thus the poet who observes the river "carrying off its lights" in a poem that ends with an intimation of human mortality in general ("Nu bærer elven sine lamper ut" ["Now the River Is Carrying Off Its Lights"]) becomes in his next book a particular person subject to the same process: "soon the river will carry off my images" ("Langsomt— —" ["Slowly— —"]).

Jacobsen's last book, *Nattåpent* (Night Watch), published in 1985, includes a suite of poems about the death of his wife, Petra, and his memo-

---

9. Borum, 37 (my translation).

Rolf Jacobsen at home, circa 1990
(photograph courtesy Trond Jacobsen and Gyldendal Norsk Forlag)

ries of their long marriage. It was probably these affecting poems that
made this book the best-selling volume of poetry Norway had seen since
the end of World War II. For Norwegian poems, they are unusually open
about private matters, including difficult feelings of grief and doubt. But
perhaps the most touching chords we hear when we read Jacobsen's late
work with his earlier work in mind are those sounded by poems that take
a personal approach to recurrent themes. For such poems have the char-
acter of summings-up in which the poet finally steps forward. In "Se opp
(OBS. OBS.)" ("Look Up [N.B. N.B.]"), Jacobsen explains why he is fond
of clouds and gray weather; in "—Mere fjell" ("—More Mountains"),
why he is content among the timeless hills. "Vi som bor ved jernbanen"
("We Who Live near the Railway") is a wonderfully relaxed poem about
a lifelong obsession. The last line of this poem illustrates Jacobsen's con-
summate way with the music of place names; but the poet goes further
still in his next book with "Hundvåko"—a poem about what place names
mean to him. In "Uten en lyd" ("Without a Sound"), Jacobsen pro-
nounces on silence itself:

What is intense has no voice.
Whatever means something. Not the dark of night.
Not the sunlight. Not death.

Luckily for us, Jacobsen dares nonetheless to give to his apprehensions of intensity and meaning a voice both precise and human.

Selection and Translation

To revised versions of the ninety-six translations in *The Silence After-wards*, which was published in 1985, this book adds twenty-one new translations included in *Did I Know You?* (1997), some of which are revised here, and four translations that have not appeared before in book form.[10] My first criterion in selecting poems has always been simply the quality of each poem in my judgment.[11] In compiling my 1985 selection, I first translated a large number of poems, then selected among them, this time on the basis of both the quality of the originals and the success of the translations as poems in English.[12] I did not set out to make the selection representative of subjects, styles, or any other features, but I was hopeful that the large number of poems would give the reader a broad, if not comprehensive, survey of Jacobsen's range.

The 1985 selection did not include poems from Jacobsen's last book, *Nattåpent* (Night Watch), which was published too late for inclusion. My translations of ten poems from that book, along with ten new translations of poems from Jacobsen's earlier books, one translation of an uncollected poem, and ten translations reprinted from the 1985 volume, appeared in *Did I Know You?* Some of the ten new pieces from Jacobsen's earlier books were translations that I had not been satisfied with at first but had managed to improve in the intervening years.

My aim in the translations has been to write good poems in English that capture the movement, tone, and to whatever degree possible, some of the texture of the originals as I interpret them, while at the same time

10. The poems appear here in the order in which they occur in the first editions of Jacobsen's books. (Editions of his collected poems preserve the same order, but omit certain poems.) There is one exception: in the selection from *Tenk på noe annet* (Think about Something Else), I have put "The Inland Line" after "'Silvery Moon,'" which follows it in all Norwegian editions.

11. After reading the article by Poul Borum that I have cited here, I went back and reconsidered several poems that he praised and that I either had not translated or had deleted. As a result, I translated and included in my 1985 selection the poem "Turnipshøst" ("Turnip Crop"), which I might otherwise have overlooked.

12. At that stage I had the valuable advice of Charles Douglas, and in a later redaction, that of Richard M. Lush.

remaining faithful to those originals' exact sense, nuances, and—again, wherever possible—ambiguities. In pursuit of this unattainable ideal I have of course tried to avoid slavish copying of Norwegian constructions, and have searched for equivalent rather than strictly parallel formulations.[13] In a few poems I felt it was essential to mimic Jacobsen's rhyming or rhythms, but I tried to write these pieces to the same standard of naturalness that governed all the others.

I have not considered it my job to "improve" the original poems (but I believe a translator should certainly do an author small favors on occasion if possible, in partial compensation for many inevitable losses). I have also tried not to impose my own stylistic preferences on them. I know, however, that I have inevitably done so to some extent, if for no other reason than that Jacobsen wrote in his language and I write in mine, and that Norwegian and English are considerably different despite their proximity on the Germanic branch of the Indo-European tree.

Where I have departed from Jacobsen's punctuation it has usually been to make intelligible in English certain relations that are discernible in Norwegian from its different conventions (the common use of commas, for example, where English calls for semicolons) or from its different syntax (for example, the inversion of subject and verb that marks, even in the absence of the usual comma, the beginning of an independent clause after a subordinate element). On rare occasions I have departed from Jacobsen's line breaks because differences in the length and weight of English equivalents made it impossible to maintain the line units supported by the Norwegian.

The reader who has no knowledge of Norwegian can do two things that will be of help in getting from the English versions as much of the feel of the originals as I have been lucky enough to capture. The first is to read *slowly*, and preferably aloud; the second is to make some attempt to approximate the Norwegian pronunciation of proper names.

Poetry in Norwegian usually moves more slowly than poetry in English—in large part because of differences between the sound qualities of the two languages. The frequency of hard consonants, the clustering of consonants, the diphthongs, and the long vowels combine to make Norwegian a language that gives one more to chew on than English does. Moreover, the large number of monosyllables and of compounded nouns frequently produces dense patterns of stresses and half-stresses, espe-

---

13. I wish to record here my debt to one of Robert Bly's translations in *Twenty Poems* (Madison, Minnesota: Seventies Press, 1977): from his version of "Solsikke" ("Sunflower") I appropriated several words and phrases that seemed happier choices than my own.

cially when a poet decides to write compactly. These two characteristics together can easily produce a caesura in a line of Norwegian poetry where the equivalent English line, even with the same number of stressed and unstressed syllables, would flow without pause.

Since Jacobsen is fond of place names and a master at employing their musical qualities, there is no way around the need to make a stab at pronouncing them with at least the right stress patterns, and if at all possible, with some approximation of their sound. Since few readers can remember and consistently apply a table of roughly equivalent sounds, I have chosen not to offer a two-page course in tongue-twisting, and instead to supply in the endnotes a phonetic transcription of each name. Most readers who have used American dictionaries will find the system of transcription familiar.

I have tried in the endnotes to supply the English-speaking reader with some of the information about background and references that a Norwegian reader might be expected to have, including those details about place names that seemed relevant to an understanding of the poems. I have also explained, for the benefit of the reader who has some access to the original, the handful of cases where it might be difficult to see how I arrived at my English versions.

I will be happy if this book leads any readers to learn enough Norwegian so that their newfound appreciation of the language makes them dissatisfied with reading translations.

The Text

The Norwegian text printed in this book is the result of a long editorial process. Rolf Jacobsen made revisions to many of his poems as successive editions of selected and collected poems appeared; at the same time, these successive editions accumulated more and more typographical errors. To establish texts for my 1985 selection, *The Silence Afterwards,* I compared *Dikt i utvalg* (Selected Poems), all the extant editions of *Samlede dikt* (Collected Poems), and the first editions of all eleven individual volumes from which the poems were drawn. I also engaged in a lengthy correspondence with Rolf Jacobsen about his revisions and about typographical and orthographical problems. Jacobsen checked proofs of the Norwegian texts printed in *The Silence Afterwards.*

In 1990 Gyldendal Norsk Forlag published *Alle mine dikt* (All My Poems), the last collected edition that Rolf Jacobsen was to oversee. Sigmund Moren acted as editor and attempted to put right some of the more egregious errors that had crept into the texts, but he did not compare first editions, and the result was not entirely satisfactory. Moreover, in spite of the book's title, Jacobsen chose to omit certain poems; what he meant by "all my poems" was "all the poems I care to include."

When I edited the Norwegian texts of the poems in *Did I Know You?* (with the benefit of advice from Morten Moi at Gyldendal), I once again compared all available editions. For one poem, "Plutselig. I desember" ("Suddenly. In December"), I had recourse to a version that had appeared in a magazine before the poem was included in Jacobsen's last individual volume, *Nattåpent* (Night Watch) in 1985 (see the endnotes for details). For the text of "Et dikt om elven Glåma" ("A Poem on the River Glåma"), which was written after the publication of *Alle mine dikt*, I relied on a volume of previously uncollected work by Jacobsen that appeared in 1996: *En liten kvast med tusenfryd og fire rare løk: Ukjente dikt og tekster 1925–1993* (A Little Cluster of Daisies and Four Strange Bulbs: Unknown Poems and Texts 1925–1993), edited by Hanne Lillebo.

In 1999, thanks to long and thorough editorial work by Hanne Lillebo, Gyldendal was finally able to do right by its great author and publish a reliable edition of *Samlede dikt* that included all the poems from his twelve original volumes, plus all the published uncollected poems that could be located. I have therefore been able to compare all the Norwegian texts in the present selection to a carefully edited edition of Jacobsen's collected poems.

This does not mean, however, that the Norwegian texts in this book are the same as those in Lillebo's edition. With a few minor exceptions, Lillebo presents the poems as they appeared in the first editions; she documents later revisions and deviations in an extensive set of endnotes. Since my goal was to supply the best reading text I could arrive at, I have usually incorporated the last revisions Jacobsen made; when I have gone back to earlier versions or have ignored or corrected changes that I judged to be inadvertent, I have noted that in my endnotes.

I have retained the Norwegian spellings I used in *The Silence Afterwards*, since I arrived at them with Jacobsen's agreement after detailed correspondence. Norway saw five official spelling reforms in the course of Jacobsen's lifetime. Under such circumstances, even the most conscientious writer could not have managed to be completely consistent. More to the point, various editors and typesetters also inevitably contributed to the inconsistencies. For the most part, I used the spelling in the first editions, as Lillebo has done. In some places, however, I changed first-edition spellings that Jacobsen agreed did not reflect his usage at the time of publication. In this way we arrived at a certain degree of orthograph-ical consistency among the poems drawn from each individual volume.

But it should be emphasized that variations often occur for poetic rea-sons. For example, an old spelling may be retained in a phrase that is quoted from or suggestive of the Bible. Sound patterns also play a role: Jacobsen uses "kolde" rather than "kalde" (cold) in "Billedhuggeren" ("The Sculptor") because this form of the word fits better among the many *o*-sounds of the first four lines (perhaps he also wished to avoid a rhyme with "all" in the next line). It emerged from his replies to my ques-tions that rhythm could also be a factor in spelling choices. For example, he connected the spelling "tunnell" with a pronunciation that stressed the second syllable (in the French manner, as he put it), and the spelling "tunnel" with a pronunciation that stressed the first syllable (in the En-glish manner—and the manner common in many eastern Norwegian dialects). In the first poem in his first book, he used both "himlen" (two syllables) and "himmelen" (three syllables), much as an English poet of an earlier era might choose, for metrical reasons, to write "blest" or "blessèd." Such considerations sometimes conflicted with Jacobsen's de-sire to modernize the spelling in his texts. In short, the textual issues in this body of work are such as to test the mettle of any editor—and to make the famously difficult spelling of English seem like a breeze.

Note to the Text

A stanza break that falls at the foot of a page is marked by the symbol ≈ near the right margin, unless it is already marked by an asterisk, dash, or section number in the poem.

NORTH IN THE WORLD
≈ ≈ ≈ ≈ ≈

fra JORD OG JERN

≈ ≈ ≈ ≈ ≈

1933

from EARTH AND IRON

≈ ≈ ≈ ≈ ≈

1933

Regn

Himlen har stillet sin harpe på skrå mot jorden
og rører de tusen strenger med døvende vellyd,
løfter de store klemt over skog og sletter
med lekende hender.

Over de nakne marker går jeg og trår på jorden
og kjenner hvor regnet driver om kneet, mulden
puster mot foten,
mens himlen legger de tynne striper av jern
tonende over mitt hjerte.

Regn var det første. Øglene bet mot regn.
Langsmed de støvgrå sumper gynget de fuktige trær.
Papegøiene kaklet. Himmelens flyvefisker
rodde sig skrikende frem
gjennem regn.

Gro, sovende land med den brune, blødende jord, gro!
Mett dig med havets såkorn, løft dig og brist
av regn.

Himmelens harpe
rører de tusen strenger, fyller det lyttende øre
med levende låt.
Over det store, syngende billedteppe
veves av milde hender, snakkende drømmer.

Regn var det første sansene skjønte på jorden
—susende regn.

Rain

The sky has rested its harp aslant on the earth
and is moving the thousands of strings in deafening harmony,
lofting great chords above forest and steppe
with playful hands.

Across the bare fields I go treading the earth
and feel how the rain drives at my knees, the loam
breathes on my foot
as the sky sets its thin iron stripes
ringing over my heart.

Rain was the first thing. The dinosaurs snapped at rain.
Humid trees swayed beside dust-gray swamps.
Parrots cackled. The flying fish of the sky
paddled forward, shrieking,
through rain.

Grow, sleeping land with your brown, bleeding earth, grow!
Eat your fill of the ocean's seed grain, swell and burst
with rain.

The sky's harp
moves the thousands of strings, fills the listening ear
with living song.
Across the great, singing tapestry
gentle hands weave speaking dreams.

Rain was the first thing the senses grasped on the earth
—rushing rain.

Myr

Spettet ut over landet ligger de gule myrer
som flekker av pest.

Gråbleke i regnet og med tåkehette brer de sin
tristhet som endeløse hav mellem tynne skoger.

Rødflammet og mosegule ligger de i solskinnet
og slikker himlen med sin tunge
av søt os.

Og noen kranser sig med unge bjerker, som
flokker av lyse piker står de og grer sitt hår
over lyngtuene.
Og noen hyller sig i en krave av brennende
blomster som de lokker til sig ut av
skogene, i en have av mjødurt, storkenebb
og hvit skogstjerne.

Og alle har de denne besettende ånde,
denne bitre lukt av søt vin. Mange mil
gjennem skogen kan jeg kjenne den som
en bedøvelse for min tanke.

Marshes

Spotted out over the land the yellow marshes lie
like patches of plague.

Sallow gray in the rain and with cowls of fog they spread their
sadness like endless seas among thin forests.

Streaked red and moss-yellow they lie in the sunshine
and lick the sky with their tongues of
sweet odor.

And some garland themselves with young birches, like
groups of fair girls they stand combing their hair
over the islets of heather.
And some wrap themselves in a collar of flaming
flowers they lure out of
the woods: in a garden of meadowsweet, cranesbill
and white wintergreen.

And they all have this engrossing breath,
this bitter smell of sweet wine. Many miles
through the forest I can feel it
anesthetizing my thought.

Skyene

Skyene ruller.
Skyene går og kommer
søvngjengerstille ut fra uendeligheten,
belte bak belte
og tog bak tog,
og skifter farve på jorden.

Og noen dager er det koldt—ett sted.
Og noen dager er det varmt—ett sted.
En dal blir rød i øst.
En dal blir blå i vest
så langt den går.

Skyene ruller.
Belte kommer bak belte
og tog bak tog
og skifter farve på jorden.

Og dagen reiser i tunnell, sånn:
—blink, blink, blink.
Og under kikhullene kommer en mann ut og sier:
«Nei for en sommer vi får.»
Og under skyggeflekkene
blir jorden grå som graven.

Skyene ruller.
Skyhavet beveger sig.
Sol-toppet,
skumrevet, hvitt
i lag på lag
og siler lyset på menneskene
og legger ny farve på deres ansikter.

Noen blir røde som blod.
Noen blir gustne som sopp i skogen.
Noen blir hvite som sne
og noen gule som honning.

The Clouds

The clouds roll on.
Silent as sleepwalkers the clouds
keep coming from infinity,
bank behind bank
and line after line,
and change colors on the earth.

And some days it's cold—somewhere.
And some days it's warm—somewhere.
A valley turns red in the east.
A valley turns blue in the west
as far as it reaches.

The clouds roll on.
Bank comes behind bank
and line after line
and change colors on the earth.

And the day travels in a tunnel, thus:
—blink, blink, blink.
And under the peepholes a man comes out and says:
"This sure will be one fine summer."
And under the shadow-patches
the earth turns gray as the grave.

The clouds roll on.
The cloud-ocean moves.
Sun-capped,
foam-reefed, white
layer upon layer.
And filters the light onto people
and sets new color on their faces.

Some become red like blood.
Some become pale like mushrooms in the forest.
Some become white like snow
and some yellow like honey.

Reise

Stasjonsventesaler om natten
med den kjølige atmosfære av rå cement
og jern,
med rekker av visnede smørbrød under
glassdiskene,
opstablede stoler i skyggen,
vaskekonenes strøm over perrongene
i den fuktige morgentime,
kan fylle min sjel med villhet.

Reise mot fremmede lande.
Røk gjennem kupévinduene, skinnenes
magiske sanger. — Paris, Marseille.

Når asfalten har krystet mine føtter
til glør,
når butikkvinduenes glitrende øine
har mistet sin trolldom
og min verden står stille og bare
stirrer på mig,
da går jeg ofte til jernbanestasjonene
hvor de hvite røksøiler setter glade
spørsmålstegn på himlen,
eller til havnen
hvor de store skib ligger med duft av
maling og hav og skinner av lys.

Jeg vil ride på stavnen av et slikt skib
inn mot en ny by.

Jeg vil høre på bølgene pusle om skrogets plater
når vi glir med sakte fart inn mot de
disige tårne og de gamle broer gjennem røk.

Og jeg vil høre gatenes larm stige,
sporvognene klemte i nye, rare toner.

Jeg vil kjenne lukten av kastanjeknopper
drive mot havnen. Kastanjeknopper og exhaust.

Travel

Station waiting rooms at night
with the cool atmosphere of raw cement
and iron,
with rows of wilted sandwiches under
glass counters,
stacked-up chairs in the shadows,
charwomen streaming down the platforms
in the damp morning hour,
can fill my soul with wildness.

Travel to foreign lands.
Smoke through compartment windows, the magic
song of the rails. — Paris, Marseilles.

When the asphalt has pressed my feet
into live coals,
when the shopwindows' glittering eyes
have lost their spell
and my world stands still and just
stares at me,
then I often go to the railway stations,
where the white columns of smoke set lively
question marks in the sky,
or to the harbor,
where the great ships lie with a fragrance of
paint and ocean, shining with lights.

I want to ride on the bow of such a ship
in toward a new city.

I want to hear the waves slosh on the hull's plates
as we glide in toward hazy towers and
old bridges at slow speed through smoke.

And I want to hear the street-noise rising,
the trolley cars clanging in new, strange notes.

I want to pick up the smell of chestnut buds
drifting toward the harbor. Chestnut buds and exhaust.

Eftermiddagen

Bilen stanser på hjørnet.
Gaten er hvit og stille.
Gardinenes dovne faner vaier
over en verden av skygge og støv.

Øde er alle spisestuer nu.
Sølvvaser glimter på røde
mahognybuffeter i halvmørke.
På tunge, svaktglødende buffeter i skygge
står kobberfat med frukt.

Nu er det at alle de selsomme mønstre våkner.
Silkeskjermenes påfugl. Broderienes blomsterakre.
Støvsylfidene leker
i skoger av ekeblader. Og fra det kinesiske tempel
strømmer det lav musikk.

Øde er alle spisestuer nu.
Det er timen da du hviler middag, borger.
Bare den store buffeten din lever
og silkeskjermen og blomstervasen.
Mens gulvteppestøvet
danser i strålen fra gatens
nytente lykter.

Båter uler på havnen.
Ute er fortauene våte.

Afternoon

A car stops at the corner.
The street is white and still.
The curtains' lazy banners flutter
over a world of shadow and dust.

All the dining rooms are empty now.
Silver vases glimmer on red
mahogany buffets in half-darkness.
On heavy, faintly shining buffets in the shadows
stand copper plates of fruit.

Now is when all the singular patterns awaken.
Peacocks on the silk screens. Embroidered fields of flowers.
The dust-sylphs play
in forests of oak leaves. And from the Chinese temple
soft music flows.

All the dining rooms are empty now.
It's the hour when you rest after dinner, burgher.
Only this big buffet of yours is alive
and the silk screen and the flower vase.
While the dust of the carpet
dances in the beam from the streetlights,
just lit.

Boats blow horns in the harbor.
Outside the sidewalks are wet.

Speilglass

På vår seilas med trikken
ut til løvetann og syriner
blev vi sittende fast i speilglass
i en lang osende kanal.
Vi la et blått kjølvann bak oss
gjennem rutenes blinkende brenning
da vi blev hyllet inn i skygge
og så var vi på byens havbund.

Over takenes bølgetopper
så vi maisolen lyse,
men i de hemmelighetsfulle sunkne paradiser
så vi unge piker av voks.

I de strålende, fortryllede akvarier
lå gaudaostenes gule møllestener,
røkelaks
og sprø, duftende roquefort med grønne perler.
Og bak de stirrende speilglass-øine
(fuktige av gatens gjennemtrekk)
korseletter, min herre,
og bysteholdere av silkerips.

La løvetannen lyse.
La trikken seile med sitt kjølvann.
—Jeg er strandet på et koralrev
og lar havets champagne bevifte mine gjellespalter.

Plate Glass

On our sailing trip by trolley
out to dandelions and lilacs
we got stuck in plate glass
in a long streaming canal.
As we left a blue wake behind us
through the glittering swell of the panes,
we were enveloped in shadow
and ended up on the city's seabed.

Above the wave-crests of the roofs
we saw the May sun shining,
but in the mysterious sunken paradise
we saw young girls of wax.

In the sparkling, bewitched aquariums
lay yellow millstones of Gouda cheese,
smoked salmon,
and crumbly, fragrant Roquefort beaded with dew.
And behind the staring plateglass eyes
(watering from the draft)
corsets, dear sir,
and brassieres of ribbed silk.

Let the dandelions shine.
Let the trolley sail on with its wake.
—I am stranded on a coral reef
and let the sea's champagne flutter the slits of my gills.

Byens metafysikk

Under rennestensristene,
under de skimlete murkjellere,
under lindealléenes fuktige røtter
og parkplenene:

Telefonkablenes nervefibre.
Gassledningenes hule blodårer.
Kloakker.

Fra østens skyhøie menneskealper,
fra vestens villafasader bak spirea
—de samme usynlige lenker av jern og kobber
binder oss sammen.

Ingen kan høre telefonkablenes knitrende liv.
Ingen kan høre gassledningenes syke hoste i avgrunnen.
Ingen kan høre kloakkene tordne med slam og stank hundrede mil
    i mørke.
Byens jernkledde innvolder
arbeider.

Men oppe i dagen danser jo du med flammende
fotsåler over asfalten, og du har silke mot navlens
hvite øie og ny kåpe i solskinnet.

Og oppe i lyset etsteds står jo jeg og ser hvordan
cigarettens blå sjel flagrer som en kysk engel
gjennem kastanjeløvet mot det evige liv.

Metaphysics of the City

Under the gutter gratings,
under the moldy stone cellars,
under the damp roots of avenues with linden trees
and the parks' lawns:

The telephone cables' nerve fibers.
The gas pipes' hollow veins.
Sewers.

From skyscraping human Alps in the east,
from spirea-hedged façades in the west
—the same invisible links of iron and copper
bind us together.

No one can hear the telephone cables' crackling life.
No one can hear the gas pipes' sick coughing in the abyss.
No one can hear the sewers thunder with slime and stench for a
    hundred miles in darkness.
The city's ironclad entrails
are at work.

But up in the day you, of course, are dancing over the asphalt
with the soles of your feet on fire, and you have silk against your
    navel's
white eye and a new coat in the sunshine.

And up in the light somewhere I, of course, stand and watch how
the cigarette's blue soul flutters like a chaste angel
through the chestnut leaves toward eternal life.

Industridistrikt

Det er i jordens oldtid

—at ditt vindu lukkes op mot morgenen
i murbergene
og knirker på sine hasper
og slipper inn lukten av kalk og ny brand
mot dine varme laken,

—at ditt øre fanger den langsomme lyd
av en dampmaskin like i nærheten,
lufthamrenes gjø over takene,
den hule hoste fra gater du ikke kan se gjennem røken,

—at ditt øie møter de store
marker av uld,
jernvanger, tomter med koks
under sparsom sol. Fabrikk-
skorstener med kroner av gul røk,

—at ditt hjerte brister i drøm:
Dinosaurene, hornøglene,
løfter de tynne halser over for-
stenede sumper
og gresser
i skyenes tak av løv,

—at din tanke med ett fylles av lys og våkner:
«Idag skal jeg ut og kjøpe nye sko.»

Industrial District

It is in the earth's prehistory

—that your window is opened to morning
amid mountains of walls
and creaks on its hinges
and lets the smell of lime and new fire drift in
toward your warm sheets,

—that your ear catches the slow sound
of a steam engine nearby,
of jackhammers barking over the roofs,
the hollow cough from streets you can't see through the smoke,

—that your eye meets the vast
fields of dust,
iron meadows, lots with coke
under thin sun. Factory
chimneys with yellow crowns of smoke,

—that your heart bursts into dream:
The dinosaurs, the horned lizards,
raise their thin necks over
petrified swamps
and graze
in the canopy of leafy clouds,

—that your mind is filled at once with light and awakens:
"Today I'm going out and buying new shoes."

Jernbaneland

1

Lysfaner henger fra kuppelen ned over boggivogntakene.
Solslyngplantene vifter sakte over kontinentaltoget.
Åtte røksorte boggier dufter cigar og mahogny.

Trallene ramler på stenen. Dampen skjuler oss alle.
Føttene klaprer, mennesker vrimler og snakker.
Veldige lokomotiver opløfter sin vrede stemme.

Strøm gjennem korridorene, tyst over gummiløpere.
Hundrede ansikter her, bak vegger av teak-tre
bleke som voks, lesende, skapt i guds billede.

Speilglassrutene klirrer, svakt knirker boggifjærene.
Snart skal hjulene spille sitt heftige accellerando.
Nu ligger de lydløst og ruger på skinnenes nakke.

*

Godsvogner. Tusen rekker
side om side i søvnen.
Tunge floder som furer
sletten av stål og jern.

Under presenninger
slåmaskiner og tømmer.
Brekkvognenes mørke gate
hvor kornet og fisken bor.

Tømmer fra duftende skoger
fløtet på langsomme elver,
hugget på moer i måneskinn
fraktet på sne.

≈

Railroad Country

Banners of light from the cupola hang down over the roofs
    of the coaches.
A foliage of heat mirages flutters slowly above the Continental.
From eight smoke-black coaches waft the scents of cigar
    and mahogany.

Baggage carts rumble on the pavements. Steam envelops everyone.
Feet clatter, people mill around talking.
Powerful locomotives raise up their angry voices.

A streaming through the corridors, muted on rubber runners.
Hundreds of faces here behind walls of teakwood,
pale as wax, reading, made in god's image.

The plateglass windows rattle, the truck-springs creak faintly.
Soon the wheels will play their mighty accelerando.
Now they sit silently brooding on the railhead.

*

Freight cars. A thousand rows
side by side, asleep.
Heavy rivers to furrow
a prairie of steel and iron.

Under tarpaulins
mowing machines and timber.
The boxcars' dark street
housing the fish and the grain.

Timber from fragrant forests
floated on leisurely rivers,
hewn in clearings by moonlight,
hauled over snow.

≈

Floder av tre, floder av jern som sover
venter på solopgangens
hvite, smeltende lys.

Da skal skredene løsne,
skinnene gjespe og sprake.
Tusen koblinger strekkes mot milenes sluk.

2

Skinnene, blinkende, brune
grener sig ut over landet
over de tjærete sviller,
gjennem de kløverrøde bakker.

Inn i de klamme tunneller
høit over klirrende broer,
gjennem den øde, ropende mo
hvor timian vifter i gruset,

og gyldenrød tiriltunge
duver ved skinnekanten.
Der snuser den røde vimsende maur
og klatrer i skinnenes rust.

Sanden ligger og lyser
med oljeflekker og mønje.
Mellem de tunge, osende sviller
vokser kamilleblomsten.

*

Det står en snehvit bue
etsteds i skogens arne
og venter med sin høie port
på hjulets kolde klang.

En ensom bro er bygget der,
en tanke spent på hvit granitt
som bærer dig i luftens blå
trygt i sitt store fang.

≈

22

Floods of wood, floods of sleeping iron
wait for the sunrise's
white, melting light.

Then the ice will loosen,
the rails will yawn and sparkle.
A thousand couplers will stretch toward the distance's maw.

2

Railroad tracks, brown-tinted, gleaming
branch their way out through the country,
over the tar-blackened crossties,
over the clover-red hillsides.

Into the long clammy tunnels,
high over rattling bridges,
crossing the empty, beckoning moor
where thyme-plants flutter in the gravel,

and golden-red babies' slippers
sway at the roadbed's border.
Poking around, the busy red ant
climbs in the rust of the tracks.

The sand is lying there shining
with red lead and oil-spots.
Between the heavy, reeking crossties
grows the camomile blossom.

*

A snow-white arch is standing
in the center of the forest,
awaiting with its lofty gate
the drive-wheels' chilly clang.

A lonely bridge constructed there,
a thought stretched out on granite, quartz,
supports you in the bluish air,
safe on its giant span.

≈

Et håndtrykk mellem bredder grå
er knyttet hett og varig her.
Et lite vers av stål og sten
i veiens store sang.

*

Inn i tunnellenes hule
følger vi skinnenes reise.
Vannet siler fra taket.
Hit kommer solen aldri.

Vannet siler fra taket
her, under Hjerpetjerns-hovet,
dråpen skraller med ekko.
Hit kommer solen aldri.

Røkens tunge vil slikke
hulens fuktige stener.
Dypt under skogenes røtter
skal sotede tak pile.

Skinnene ligger og venter
boltet og spent over pukksten.
Vannet plasker på svillen.
Hit kommer solen aldri.

3

Slik er skinnegangen spent over jorden som en bro.
Slik er hjulenes søvn i den nattlige havn.
Men når dagen bryter frem og når det lysner over mo
skal de grådige åpne sin favn.

Da skal de møtes i en dans, da skal de sprenge sin lyd
i et jagende ridt gjennem skoger og fjell.
Da skal et tusentunget rop som en jublende koral
bryte frem over hjulets propell.

≈

The handshake of the two gray cliffs
is sealed here ardently, for good.
A little verse of steel and stone
in the railway's mighty song.

*

Into the caves of the tunnels
we follow the rails on their journey.
Water drips from the ceiling.
Here sunlight never enters.

Water drips from the ceiling
here, under Hjerpetjern Mountain,
droplets clatter with echoes.
Here sunlight never enters.

Tongues of smoke will lap at
the dripping rock of the cavern
when sooty roofs go scooting
under the roots of forests.

The rails are lying there waiting
bolted and tensed over gravel.
Water splashes on crossties.
Here sunlight never enters.

3

That's how the rail line is stretched like a bridge across the earth.
Such is the sleep of the wheels in their haven at night.
But as soon as daybreak comes and it lightens on the heath
the greedy cars will open for freight.

Then they will meet in a dance, then they will blast out their sound
in a galloping ride across forests and hills.
Then a thousand-tongued cry like a joyous chorale
will break out above the whirr of the wheels.

≈

Og hver time på dag og hvert eneste minutt
skal vår jord veltes rundt av den spillende plog.
Og du møter dem ved natt når de skjærer med sitt lys
som en flaggermusving gjennem skog.

Jeg har sovet i et hus som lå like ved en vei
hvor de støvede hurtigtog jager forbi.
Jeg har lyttet til en sang som har dryppet i mitt sinn
en besettende, vill melodi.

Jeg har stanset mine skritt, jeg har stoppet for å se
når den smekre maskin med den glinsende buk
kom og trommet med sin hov over miler av metall
på sitt ridt mot det blinkende sluk.

Jeg har lyttet til dens rop og den kaller mig ved navn
og den kommer til mitt hus som min daglige gjest
og den sier til mitt sinn, du skal selge hvad du har,
være fri som den jagende blest.

For det kommer nok en dag og det kommer nok en tid
da den jord hvor du trår er en brennende jord.
Og du rømmer fra dig selv og da kommer du til mig
på min flukt over syngende spor.

Og du finner ikke ro og du leter overalt
gjennem tider og land i en rivende strøm.
Og du hører mine hjul som en tromme i ditt blod
på din jakt mot den ytterste drøm.

Jeg har sovet i et hus som lå like ved en vei
hvor de gyngende hurtigtog hamrer forbi.
Jeg har lyttet til en sang som har hugget i mitt sinn
en forheksende, vill melodi.

Og jeg hører den ved dag og jeg hører den ved natt
som en bankende knoke av stål på min port.
Og jeg drømte det inatt, og jeg trodde det var sant
at jeg stengte min dør og gikk bort.

And each hour by day and each minute by the clock
our earth will be plowed by that musical blade.
And you'll meet it at night when it slices with its beam
like the wing of a bat through the glade.

I have slept in a house that stood just beside a line
where the dusty expresses come racing the grade.
I have listened to a song that has dripped into my mind
an obsessive and wild serenade.

I have stopped in my tracks, I have halted to look
when the slender machine with the glistening ribs
came drumming on its hoofs over endless miles of steel
on its ride toward the flashing abyss.

I have listened to its cry and it calls to me by name
and it comes to my house every day like a friend
and it whispers to my mind, you shall sell what you own,
and be free as the scudding wind.

For there will surely come a day and there will surely come a time
when the earth underfoot will be burning coals.
And you'll flee from yourself and then you'll come to me
in my flight over singing rails.

And you won't find any peace, you'll be searching everywhere
across ages and lands: a torrential stream.
And you'll listen to my wheels like a drumming in your blood
while you hunt for the ultimate dream.

I have slept in a house that stood just beside a line
where the rocking expresses come pounding the grade.
I have listened to a song that has chiseled in my mind
a bewitching and wild serenade.

And I hear it by day and I hear it at night
like a knuckle of steel rapping urgent and rough.
And I dreamt it tonight, and I thought it was real:
that I shut my door and walked off.

fra VRIMMEL

≈ ≈ ≈ ≈ ≈

1935

from SWARM

≈ ≈ ≈ ≈ ≈

1935

Nordlyset

Dagen som stiger med gråt i halsen
bak raggete horisonter er ikke
en virkelig dag, men
alle de døde
forstøtte dager som ikke fant frem til et hjerte.
Nødens dager, sultens og frostens, som
lurer sig hit om natten og prøver
å skinne litt sol og strømme litt lys
fra hungrende, visne bryst.

Fryktsom løfter den
ansiktet nu bak hundrede skoger
og stirrer med brennende øine
ut over riker den ikke fikk lov til å elske.

Nu beveger den sine fingre
og rusker i de svarte sprinkler av natt
og forsøker atter og atter å tende sin osende sol,
men den visner,
svinner og blåses ut av kulden.
Langt ut i vest—ytterst i øst
forsøker den å slippe igjennem, men nattens
murer er bygget av granitt
og dens søiler av stål.

Stirr gjennem rutene,
kom barhodet ut på veiene, og stå
i klynger ved veikryssene:
Langsomt synker den kjempendes armer.
Stum river hun sine klær i stykker,
brenner dem så på
kuldens strålende bål.
Røken
blusser op over skogene.
Røken

The Northern Lights

The day that rises with tears in its throat
behind shaggy horizons is not
a real day, but
all the dead
disowned days that didn't make it into anyone's heart.
Days of need, of hunger and chill, which
sneak back here at night and try
to shine a little sun and pour a little light
from starving, withered breasts.

Timidly it raises
its face now behind a hundred forests
and stares with burning eyes
out over kingdoms it wasn't allowed to love.

Now it moves its fingers
and shakes night's black picket fence
and tries again and again to kindle a smoldering sun
that fades,
dwindles and is blown out by the cold.
Far out in the west—far off to the east
it tries to slip through, but the night's
walls are built of granite
and its pillars of steel.

Stare through the panes,
come out on the roads bareheaded, and stand
in clusters at the crossroads:
Slowly the struggler's arms sink down.
In silence she rips her clothes to pieces,
then burns them on
the cold's brilliant bonfire.
The smoke
blazes up over the forests.
The smoke

slår ned over grantoppene og de lave huser på moene.
Røken
fryser til is på himlen, så morgendagen
får grimer av gråt.

blows down over the tops of spruce and the low houses
　　on the moors.
The smoke
freezes to ice in the sky, so tomorrow
is streaked gray with weeping.

Gummi

En hvit morgen i juni klokken fire
da landeveiene ennu var grå og våte
gjennem skogenes uavladelige tunneller,
hadde det gått en bil over støvet
der hvor mauren kom syslende ut med sin barnål nu,
og blev vandrende rundt i det store G i «Goodyear»
som stod presset i landeveissandet
over et hundre og tyve kilometer.
Furunåler er tunge.
Gang på gang gled den med sin vippende last
tilbake
og arbeidet sig op igjen
og skled tilbake igjen.
På reisen frem over det store, skybelyste Sahara.

Rubber

One pale morning in June at four o'clock
when the country roads were still gray and wet
in their endless tunnels of forest,
a car had passed over the clay
just where the ant came out busily with its pine needle now
and kept wandering around in the big G of "Goodyear"
that was imprinted in the sand of country roads
for a hundred and twenty kilometers.
Pine needles are heavy.
Time after time with its load tottering it slid
back down
and worked its way up again
and slipped back again.
Outward bound across the great, cloud-illumined Sahara.

Europa

Et ansikt kommer frem av Asia med munnen
åpen og håret kastet tilbake.

Og lar sig kjærtegne av vinden, mens det ler
mot bølgene og snuser inn smaken av salt
som strømmer inn fra de blå sletter.

Dag og natt kan vi høre dets latter fra
kystene: Truende og eftertenksom, spottende
og underfundig, omtrent som den henvendte sig
til noen—vinden, skyene eller til de små
stener som ligger og slipes runde av brenningen.

Europe

A face emerges from Asia with its mouth
open and hair thrown back.

And lets the wind caress it, while it laughs
toward the waves and sniffs the flavor of salt
that streams in from the blue plains.

Day and night we can hear its laughter from
the coasts: threatening and pensive, derisive
and clever, almost as if it were addressed
to someone—the wind, the clouds or the small
stones being polished round by the breakers.

Arv og miljø

Uskyldig
med store pupiller
og forskrekkede øienbryn
og munnen nysgjerrig spiss
som et barn
går hun til dans
under glatte projektører, kjelne projektører.
Tango og
Cucaracha
til kastanjetter, slik:
Armene løftet. To skritt til siden.
Knekke klosset i knærne.

Nu stirrer
med uskyldige pupiller
og forskrekkede øienbryn
gassmasken ut over verden
med sin snabel nysgjerrig spiss
som et barn.

Så går vi til dans
under kolde projektører, hvite projektører.
Tango og
Cucaracha
til mitraljøser, slik:
Armene løftet. To skritt til siden.
Knekke klosset i knærne.

Heredity and Environment

Innocently
with large pupils
and frightened eyebrows
and her mouth a curious pout
like a child
she begins to dance
under slick spotlights, soft spotlights.
Tango and
Cucaracha
to castanets, like this:
Arms raised. Two steps to the side.
Awkwardly buckling knees.

Now
with innocent pupils
and frightened eyebrows
the gas mask stares out over the world
with its snout a curious point
like a child.

Then we begin to dance
under cold spotlights, white spotlights.
Tango
and Cucaracha
to machine guns, like this:
Arms raised. Two steps to the side.
Awkwardly buckling knees.

Dirrende telefonstolper

Lyden av stjernenes tunge kvernstener
som skurer langsomt omkring de veldige nav, og
vender de rimfrosne ansikter mot hverandre
og bøier dem bort igjen bak millioner mil,
—alt som beveger sig ute i verdensrummet
på gigantiske kulelagre, utsender lave lyder,
pipende sang som dør av de store avstander.
Dette er det vi hører i bruset fra telefontrådene,
de er antenner som innfanger rummets signaler
og roper dem ut på øde moer om natten
når stolpene står og murrer og kaller urolig
som når et menneske drømmer mørke drømmer
og noe biter i hjertet, kvalfulle tanker
han ikke skjønner, som baner sig vei gjennem strupen,
men stanses av ganen og blir bare brutte rop,
da er det lyden av alle stjernene,
slik tuter det alltid ute i verdensrummet.

Vibrating Telephone Poles

The sound of the stars' heavy millstones
that scrape slowly around their huge hubs, and
turn their hoarfrosted faces toward each other
and bend them away again behind a million miles
—everything that moves in outer space
on gigantic ball bearings transmits faint sounds,
a whining song that dies out in the great distances.
This is what we hear in the hum from telephone wires,
they are antennas that capture the signals from space
and cry them out over desolate moors at night
when the poles are murmuring and calling anxiously
as when a person dreams dark dreams
and something bites his heart, agonizing thoughts he
doesn't understand, that force their way through his throat,
but are stopped by the roof of his mouth and become only
     broken cries,
that is the sound of the stars,
that's how it always howls in outer space.

fra FJERNTOG

≈ ≈ ≈ ≈ ≈

1951

from EXPRESS TRAIN

≈ ≈ ≈ ≈ ≈

1951

Gasslys

Nu blomstrer poteten. Den har tent lys i sine gater,
ringlende rader av lys i de endeløse alleer
i de store byer med kjellerne stentunge av mat.
Fjern, fjern hvitner månen nu i hvelvene
og bakkene blekner den i møte
med dette lyshav, disse millioner gasslys flimrende
i uendelige boulevarder langt borte
hvor ingen klokker ringer og alle tog står stille
—i de grønne byer med kjellerne mørke av mat.

Gaslight

Now the potato plants are flowering. They've lit up their streets,
rows of whispering lights down endless avenues
in great cities whose cellars are rock-solid with food.
Remote, the moon is growing whiter in its vault,
and the hills shine back faintly
with this sea of lights, these millions of flickering gas-lamps
on unending boulevards, far off
where no bells ring and no trains run
—in those green cities, cellars dark with food.

Koks

Det raste i koksbøttene
og vi fyrte ovnene med larm dengang,
med lyn og torden morgen, middag og kveld,
og på gatene ramlet hjul med svære aksler,
dundret umåtelig høyt hestevognene.
Det luktet kokegass og fetevarer i Kristiania.
Og koks.

Det var i en damp-tid. Under dens hvite pinsehegger mot himlen
og mellem røksøylenes mørke stammer var jeg barn. I deres skoger
fant jeg de første kalde blomster: Koks
i Teatergaten.

Coke

A rushing in the coke-scuttles
and we fired the stoves with a racket back then,
with lightning and thunder morning, noon and night,
and wheels with massive axles rumbled in the streets,
the horse-drawn wagons roared terribly loud.
It smelled of cooking-gas and pork in Kristiania.
And coke.

It was an Age of Steam. Under the white cherry blossoms it sent
    toward the sky
and between the dark trunks of its columns of smoke, I had my
    childhood. In their forests
I found the first cold flowers: coke
in Theater Street.

Kobolt

Farvene er ordenes små søstre. De kan ikke bli soldater.
Hemmelig har jeg elsket dem lenge.
De skal holde sig ved husene og henge opp de klare gardiner
om vår hverdags kammers, kjøkken og alkove.

Den unge Karmosin står mig meget nær, og den brune Sienna
men ennu mere den tenksomme Kobolt med de fjerne øyne og det
    ubetråtte sind.
Vi går i dugg.
Nattehimlen og de sydlige hav
er hennes eiendeler
og et tåresmykke om panden:
Cassiopeias perler.
Vi går i dugg i sene netter.

Men de andre.
Møt dem en junimorgen klokken fire,
når de kommer stormende dig i møte
til morgenbadet i de grønne vikers skum.
Så kan du sole dig med dem på svabergene.
    —Hvem vil du eie?

Cobalt

Colors are words' little sisters. They can't become soldiers.
I've loved them secretly for a long time.
They have to stay home and hang up the sheer curtains
of our familiar kitchen, bedroom and den.

I'm very close to young Crimson, and brown Sienna
but even closer to thoughtful Cobalt with her distant eyes
    and untrampled spirit.
We walk in dew.
The night sky and the southern ocean
are her possessions
and a tear-shaped pendant on her forehead:
the pearls of Cassiopeia.
We walk in dew on late nights.

But the others.
Meet them on a June morning at four o'clock
when they come rushing toward you,
on your way to a morning swim in the green cove's spray.
Then you can sunbathe with them on the smooth rocks.
    —Which one will you make yours?

Solsikke

Hvilken såmann gikk over Jorden,
hvilke hender sådde
hjertenes frøkorn av ild?

Som regnbuens striper gikk de av hans never
til tæle, ung muld, het sand,
der skal de sove
grådig, og drikke vårt liv
og sprenge det i stumper
for en solsikkes skyld som du ikke kjenner
eller en tistelkrone eller en krysantemum.

Kom tårers unge regn,
kom sorgs milde hender.
Det er ikke så ondt som du tror.

Sunflower

What sower walked over the Earth,
which hands sowed
our hearts' kernels of fire?

Like rainbow bands they went out from his fists
to frozen soil, young loam, hot sand;
there they will sleep,
voracious, and drink our life
and blast it to pieces
for the sake of a sunflower you don't know about
or a thistle head or a chrysanthemum.

Come, young rain of tears;
come, gentle hands of sorrow.
It's not as terrible as you think.

Fjerntog

Fjerntoget 1256 jager langs bortgjemte, avlåste grender. Hus efter
hus vandrer forbi, gråbleke, hutrende. Skigarder, knauser og sjø og
de lukkede grindene.
   Da må jeg tenke i morgendemringen: Hva ville skje om noen fikk
åpne for hjertenes ensomhet? Mennesker bor der, ingen kan se dem,
de går over gulvene, inne bak dørene, nøden, stengte i øynene, hårde
av elskov de ikke kan gi og som ingen får gi dem.
Hva ville stige høyere her enn fjellene,—Skarvangkampene,
hvilken flamme, hvilken kraft, hvilke stormer av rolig lys?

Fjerntoget 1256, åtte sotsvarte boggier,
svinger mot nye, ustanselig ukjente grender.
Kilder av lys bak rutene, usette brønner av kraft langsmed fjellene
reiser vi forbi, haster vi forbi, bare fire minutter forsinket
til Marnardal.

Express Train

Express train 1256 races alongside hidden, remote villages. House after house wanders by, pale gray, shivering. Rail fences, rocks and lakes, and the closed gates.

Then I have to think in the morning twilight: What would happen if someone could release the loneliness of those hearts? People live there, no one can see them, they walk across rooms, in behind the doors, the need, blank-eyed, hardened by love they cannot give and no one gets a chance to give them.
What would rise higher here than the mountains—the Skarvang
    Hills—
what flame, what force, what storms of steady light?

Express train 1256, eight soot-black cars,
turns toward new, endlessly unknown villages.
Springs of light behind the windows, unseen wells of power along
    the mountains—
these we travel past, hurry past, only four minutes late
for Marnardal.

Mitt tre

Eneren, lyngens mor, er mitt tre.
Den trenger ingen sommer, bare regn og sne.

Fillet krone den løfter, ingen har hørt dens sus.
Den har en lang, seig rot som kan gro av grus.

Den bærer vind over skuldrene, skyene i sitt hår.
Den kan stå i stormen. Knelende. Men den står.

Kanskje den har en drøm i sindet: Det hvite ranunkel-bed
der verden slutter og breene kommer ned.

Av alle trær på jorden nærmest den store sne,
breenes blinde sol. Å, var jeg som det.

My Tree

Juniper, heather's mother, is my tree.
No summer—rain and snow are all it needs.

It lifts a ragged crown: no one has heard its rustle.
It has a long, tough root that can grow in gravel.

It wears wind on its shoulders, in its hair the clouds.
It can hold in storms. Kneeling. But it holds.

Perhaps it has a dream in mind: the white crow-foot bed
where the world stops and the glaciers descend.

Closest of all trees on earth to the great snow,
the glacier's blind sun. Oh, to be one of them.

Dagen og natten

Endeløs er vår dag.
Den er uten ende.
Den går bare bort til et annet sted,
flytter sig stille bort en liten stund,
slår den blå kåpen omkring sine skuldre,
skyller føttene i havet og går bort,
så kommer den løpende tilbake igjen, med roser på kinn,
og med svale, gode hender
løfter den din hake opp og ser dig inn i ansiktet:
—Er du våken snart?

Endeløs er vår natt.
Den er uten ende.
Den går bare bort til et annet sted
en liten stund,
så er den der igjen
med sine feberøyne
og håret dryppende vått som av sved
og ser på dig, og ser på dig:
—Hvorfor sover du ikke?

Det er ingen ende på fryden, ikke på smerten,
ikke på døden, ikke på livet.
De går bare bort en liten stund, de går rundt jorden
til et annet hjerte,
en liten stund,
så kommer de igjen, med sine nølende stemmer:
—Sover du? Er du våken?

Det er ingen ende på stjernene og på vinden.
Det er bare du selv
som ikke er den du tror.

Day and Night

Our day is endless.
It is without end.
It just goes off to another place,
moves off quietly for a little while,
throws the blue coat around its shoulders,
rinses its feet in the ocean and walks off;
then it comes running back again, with roses on its cheeks,
and with good, cool hands
it lifts up your chin and looks you in the face:
—Will you be waking soon?

Our night is endless.
It is without end.
It just goes off to another place
for a little while,
then it's there again
with its feverish eyes
and its hair dripping as if with sweat
and looks at you, and looks at you:
—Why aren't you sleeping?

There is no end to delight, none to pain,
none to death, none to life.
They just go off for a little while, they go around the earth
to another heart,
for a little while,
then they come back, with their hesitant voices:
—Are you asleep? Are you awake?

There is no end to the stars and the wind.
There is only you yourself,
who aren't who you think you are.

På Varaldskogen

Der var i den nedre natten, da lyset rant ut mellem skogens søyler
og Verdensaltet med ett var kommet helt hit ned til Varildbakken
med svart natt helt fra disse grindstolper og frem til Sirius
     og Capella,
da sprang det en stjerne frem fra Lebbikø, og enda en fra
     Jakobsbakken,
lik en blank nagle slått inn i natten,
og en til
og enda en på nytt berg lenger ut,
at livet skulde bæres frem
ennu en tid.

Og slik, i svart tordnende skog, hvor elg stod nær,
så jeg dem springe frem, en for en, parafinstjernene
i endeløst fjerne berg, og jeg visste da
at slik sprang de frem nu gjennem Gudbrandsdalen
og et lite lys ute på Grip, og i rare mønstre over Nord-Fosen og
     gjennem Bykle-hei,
og jeg så for første gang hvor stort mørket var.

Hvor stort mørket var rundt menneskene, der ensomme billykter
     kom og gikk, som kometene,
sopende sin lyskvast gjennem skoger,
tentes og sluktes ut.

Jeg hilser dere små lys fra Sarjalampi, Vais, Kvindegardslii,
     Vinjebygd,
når lyset er nesten fortapt og bare dette spinkle grindsle er igjen
mellem oss og døden,
hilser dere som naglene i vår høye bro gjennem natten
fra kyst til kyst.

Jeg hilser dere lys fra Orion, Antares, Alfa i Centauren,
men hør:

In the Varald Forest

It was the underside of night, when the light gave out between
    the forest's columns
and suddenly the Universe had come all the way down here
    to Varild Hill
with black night straight from these gateposts out to Sirius and
    Capella;
then a star leapt out from Lebbikø, and yet another from
    Jakobsbakken,
like a shiny rivet shot into the night,
and one more
and still another on a new mountain further out,
that life might be carried on
for another while.

And thus, in black thundering forest, where moose stood close by,
I saw them leap forth, one by one, the paraffin stars
on endless distant mountains, and I knew then
that they were springing up now throughout the Valley of
    Gudbrandsdal
and a small light out at Grip, and in strange patterns across North
    Fosen and all through Bykle-hei,
and I saw for the first time how great the darkness was.

How great the darkness was around people, where lonely
    headlights came and went, like the comets,
sweeping their tuft of light through forests,
were lit and were snuffed out.

I salute you, small lights from Sarjalampi, Vais, Kvindegardslii,
    hamlet of Vinje,
when the light is almost lost and only this flimsy shield of a gate
    is left
between us and death;
salute you as the rivets in our lofty bridge across the night
from coast to coast.

I salute you, lights from Orion, Antares, Alpha Centauri,
but hear me:

—når jordens bleke stjerner lover dag,
hva lover så Galaksens stjernesky,
Syvstjernens ris og Kosmos tåreslør?
Hva stiger der for glans av neste gry,
hva venter der for dag ved nattens dør?

—If the pallid stars of Earth can promise day,
what's pledged by the Galactic cloud of stars,
the Pleiades, the Cosmic mist of tears?
What brilliance of what rising dawn is theirs,
what day is waiting there for night to clear?

fra HEMMELIG LIV
≈ ≈ ≈ ≈ ≈

1954

from SECRET LIFE

≈ ≈ ≈ ≈ ≈

1954

Pavane

Pavanen, denne sære påfugldansen
som infantinnen Isabella danset
med don Juan Fernandez av Castilien
den siste natt før døden gjestet slottet
— likblek og merket alt av kalde fingrer
men kledt i påfuglprakt og med de stive
bizarre skritt som om de alt var døde
— den samme dans som Spanias dronning danset
med hjertet tungt av frykt og halvt forstenet
av tung brokade, pomp og etikette
lik hård emalje om det ville hjertet,
— er det den samme dans som havet danser
med skyene derute, denne stumme
forstemte lek med skyers påfuglhaler
og havets brutte skritt i tung brokade
mot øde himmelhvelv — slik danser havet
til dump musikk en ødslig dans med skyer.

Pavane

Pavane, unique outlandish dance of peacocks
the Infanta Isabella danced for hours
with Captain Juan Fernandez of Castilla
the evening death came calling at the palace
— pale as corpses, marked by chilly fingers
yet clothed in peacock splendor, with macabre
and stiffened steps as if they'd died already
— the dance the Queen of Spain was also dancing
with heavy, frightened heart and almost frozen
by dense brocade and pomp and courtly manners
around her untamed heart like hard enamel
— is that the very dance the sea is dancing
together with the clouds out there, this muted
and doleful play: the clouds with tails of peacocks,
the sea in dense brocade with broken movements,
a barren sky — that's how the sea is dancing
a dismal dance with clouds to muffled music.

Landskap med gravemaskiner

De spiser av skogene mine.
Seks gravemaskiner kom og spiste av skogene mine.
Gud hjelpe mig for en skapning på dem. Hoder
uten øyne og øynene i baken.

De svinger med kjeftene på lange skaft
og har løvetann i munnvikene.

De eter og spytter ut, spytter ut og eter,
for de har ingen strupe mer, bare en diger
kjeft og en rumlende mave.
Er dette et slags helvete?

For vadefugler. For de altfor kloke
pelikaner?

De har blindede øyner og lenker om føttene.
De skal arbeide i århundrer og tygge blåklokkene
om til asfalt. Dekke dem med skyer av fet exhaust
og kald sol fra projektører.

Uten struper, uten stemmebånd og uten klage.

Landscape with Steam Shovels

They're eating up my woods.
Six steam shovels came and started eating up my woods.
God help me! what creatures they are. Heads
without eyes and eyes in their rumps.

They swing their jaws on long shafts,
dandelions in the corners of their mouths.

They eat and spit out, spit out and eat,
for they have no throats, just enormous
jaws and rumbling stomachs.
Is this some sort of hell—

for wading birds? For the far too wise
pelicans?

They have blinded eyes and chains around their feet.
They will work for centuries and chew the bluebells
into asphalt, cover them with clouds of greasy exhaust
and cold sun from floodlights.

Without throats, without vocal cords, and without complaint.

De store symfoniers tid

De store symfoniers tid
er over nu.

De steg mot himlen i stor prakt
som solskimrende skyer med torden i
over de store århundrer.
Cumulus under lyshimler. Coriolan.

Nu strømmer de ned igjen som regn,
et stengrått, stripet regn over alle bølgelengder og programmer
og dekker jorden som en våt frakk, en sekk av lyd.

Nu faller de ned igjen fra himlen,
de pisker mot skyskraperne som elektrisk hagl
og drypper ned i bondens kammers
og trommer over villabyene og murstenshavet
som evindelig lyd.

Regn som lyd.
Seid umschlungen Millionen,
til å døve skrik

alle dager, alle dager
over jorden som er tørst og tar dem til sig igjen.

The Age of the Great Symphonies

The age of the great symphonies
is over now.

They rose toward the heavens in full splendor
like thunderclouds shimmering in the sun
over the great centuries.
Cumulus under clear skies. Coriolanus.

Now they're pouring back down as rain,
a stone-gray, streaked rain on all wavelengths and programs,
covering the earth like a wet coat, a sack of sound.

Now they're falling back down from the heavens,
they pelt the skyscrapers like electric hail
and seep down into the farmer's bedroom
and drum on the suburbs and the oceans of brick
as continuous sound.

Rain as sound.
Seid umschlungen Millionen,
to deaden screams

every day, every day
on this earth that is thirsty and drinks them in again.

Den ensomme veranda

Langt inne høyt oppe i en stor by hang en ensom veranda,
oppe under skyene hos vinden og som aldri noe menneske hadde
   satt sin fot på
fordi det var så dypt ned og så kaldt derute.

Den syntes den var den ensomste veranda i hele verden
og den hørte på klokkespillet hver søndag fra den hellige
   Bartholomeus' kirke,
og den tenkte hvorfor kan ikke den gode Gud hjelpe mig,
han er jo også høyt oppe
og han kunde bruke mig som en liten hylle til å legge sine
   små ting på.
Vestenvinden kjente den best, så bad den vinden spørre.

Da kom et veldig stålstillas og klatrende menn en dag
og de hugget den ned med acetylenflamme på mindre enn
   8 minutter
og hengte opp en sprakende lysreklame i rødt og blått
for Skotsk Whisky.

The Lonely Balcony

Once upon and high atop a big city hung a lonely balcony,
up under the clouds with the wind, that no person had ever
    set foot on
because it was so cold out there and such a long way down.

It thought it was the loneliest balcony in the whole world
and it heard the carillon playing every Sunday from Saint
    Bartholomew's Church,
and it thought why can't the good Lord help me,
he too after all is high up
and he could use me as a little shelf to put his knickknacks on.
It knew the western wind best, so asked that wind to inquire.

Then huge steel scaffolds and clambering men appeared one day
and they cut it down with acetylene torches in less than 8 minutes
and hung up a crackling red and blue neon advertisement
for Scotch Whiskey.

Arkeologen

Han skar torven ut med skarp spade
og gravde stenene frem med spiseskjeer
til hjørnene av en boplass kom frem
og restene av et sverd
under falmet aske.

Og det var en grønn og god dag der i skogen,
og da han spiste sine påsmurte rundstykker
tenkte han langsomt mens han tygget at det var
sitt eget hjerte han gravde ut idag
med barneskjeer.

Murrestene han støtte på under der
og stenhjørnet under askelaget
hadde han støtt panden mot før
og fått snudd veiene sine,
hver gang han trodde det skulde gå ham godt i verden.

For det har bodd noen før, tenkte han
dypt nede i mørket mitt.
Det er merkene efter dem
og hellene de la huset på
som er skjebnen min.

Det har bodd noen før i mig
    Ne's sólu sótt ok ne saxi
    steinn skorinn
som i alle mørker og menn.

Han fant også et smykke der med en liten fugl på
og et kjeveben av en hest.

Senere gravde han frem en paraply
fra en tid de ikke hadde paraplyer,
og en månedsbillett til Blommenholm
men den var visst hans egen.

The Archaeologist

He cut out the peat with a sharp spade
and exposed the stones with tablespoons
till the corners of a settlement emerged
and the remains of a sword
under faded ash.

And it was a good green day in the forest,
and when he ate his homemade sandwiches
he thought slowly as he chewed that it was
his own heart he was digging up today
with teaspoons.

The crumbled walls he came upon down there
and the stone corner under the layer of ash—
he had bumped his head against them before,
and gotten turned back
each time he thought that things would go well for him
    in the world.

For people, he thought, have lived deep down
in my darkness before me.
The marks they left behind
and the flat rocks they set their house on
are my fate.

Someone has lived in me before
    Ne's sólu sótt ok ne saxi
    steinn skorinn
as in all darknesses and men.

He also found there a piece of jewelry with a little bird on it
and a jawbone from a horse.

Later he dug up an umbrella
from an era when they didn't have umbrellas,
and a monthly rail-pass to Blommenholm
but that was surely his own.

Tømmer

Det er godt det finnes tømmer enda i verden
og velteplasser nok
enda.
For det er en stor fred i tømmeret
og et stort lys i det
som kan skinne langt inn i kveldene
om sommeren.

Det er god trøst i bråterøk
og i god kvae som trenger ut i store perler
dypt inni skogene.
Lukten av tømmer minner om søt valmue og korn.

Det er godt det lyser av tømmer nok på moene enda
ved Ångermanelven og Deep Creek, Columbia,
som en søle efter solstrålene
rundt om i verden,
en sovende styrke på jorden, en hemmelig kraft
som skal vare i slektsledd, nesten som jern.

Det har brødets farve og kvinnekroppens
og den skinnende viljen i sig
som kanskje kommer av stor kjærlighet.

For tømmeret er en del av den store våren i verden.
Det kommer fra kilder som ødeleggeren enda ikke har nådd.

————

Det er de store elvene som tar sig av det.
Er det en elskov mellem treets kraft og vannets?
De fører det sakte rundt store nes i en stille rytme som minner
    om dans.

————

Det er disse ting stjernehimmelen er satt over:
De dødes ensomhet, ungdommens mot og tømmer
som føres langsomt avsted på store elver.

Timber

It's good that timber is still there in the world,
and there are still enough places
for stacking it up.
For there is a great peace in timber
and a great light in it
that can shine far into the evenings
in summertime.

There is good solace in smoke from brushwood
and in rich sap that wells out in big pearls
deep in the forests.
The smell of timber recalls sweet poppies and grain.

It's good that the clearings from the Ångerman River to
Deep Creek, Columbia still shine
with timber like a slick of sunbeams
all around the world,
a sleeping force on earth, a secret power
that will last for generations, almost like iron.

It has the color of bread and of women's bodies
and contains the shining will
that likely stems from great love.

For timber is part of the great Spring in the world.
It comes from sources the ravager still hasn't reached.

————

The large rivers look after it.
Is this an embrace between the wood's power and the water's?
They lead it slowly round high headlands in a calm rhythm
    that reminds one of dance.

————

These are the things the starry sky is set above:
loneliness of the dead, courage of youth, and timber
that's carried slowly away on great rivers.

Skytsengelen

Jeg er fuglen som banker på vinduet til dig om morgenen
og følgesvennen din, han du ikke kan vite,
blomstene som lyser for den blinde.

Jeg er brekronen over skogene, den blendende
og malmstemmene fra katedralenes tårn.
Tanken som plutselig faller ned over dig midt på dagen
og fyller dig med en besynderlig lykke.

Jeg er en du har elsket for lenge siden.
Jeg går ved siden av dig om dagen og ser ufravendt på dig
og legger munnen på hjertet ditt,
men du vet det ikke.

Jeg er den tredje armen din og den andre
skyggen din, den hvite,
som du ikke har hjerte til
og som ikke kan glemme dig mere.

Guardian Angel

I am the bird that knocks at your window in the morning
and your companion, whom you cannot know,
the blossoms that light up for the blind.

I am the glacier's crest above the forests, the dazzling one
and the brass voices from cathedral towers.
The thought that suddenly comes over you at midday
and fills you with a singular happiness.

I am one you have loved long ago.
I walk alongside you by day and look intently at you
and put my mouth on your heart
but you don't know it.

I am your third arm and your second
shadow, the white one,
whom you don't have the heart for
and who cannot ever forget you.

De gamle damer

De unge kvinnene med lynsnare føtter, hvor blir det av dem,
De som har knær som små kyss og sovende hår?

Langt ute i tiden når de er blitt stille
gamle damer med smale hender og går langsomt i trappene

med store nøkler i vesken og ser sig omkring
og snakker til små barn ved kirkegårdsportene.

I det fremmede store landet hvor vintrene er lange
og ingen mere skjønner deres sprog.

Bøy dig dypt og hils dem med ærbødighet for
de bærer det med sig enda som en duft,

et hemmelig bitt i kinnet, en nerve inne i
håndflatene etsteds som røper dem.

The Old Ladies

The young women with lightning-quick feet—what becomes
     of them?
The ones who have knees like small kisses, and sleeping hair.

Much further along when they've become quiet
old ladies with slender hands and go slow on the stairs

with huge keys in their bags, and look around
and talk to little children by the churchyard gates.

In the vast foreign country where the winters are long
and no one understands their language anymore.

Bow deeply and greet them with respect, for
they carry it with them still, like a fragrance,

a hidden bite inside their cheeks, a nerve deep in
their palms somewhere that gives them away.

Alderdommen

Jeg holder mere av de gamle.
De sitter og ser på oss og ser oss ikke
og har nok med sitt eget,
som fiskere langs store elver,
stille som sten
i sommernatten.
Jeg holder meget av fiskere langs elver
og gammelt folk og de som kommer ut efter lang sykdom.

De har noe i øynene
som verden ikke ser lenger
de gamle, lik rekonvalesenter
som føttene ikke er sterke nok under enda
og med bleke pander som efter feber.

De gamle
som blir sig selv igjen langsomt
og løses opp langsomt,
som en røk, umerkelig går de over
i søvn
og lys.

Old Age

My heart's with the old folks.
They sit looking at us and don't see us
and are content on their own,
like fishermen along big rivers,
still as stone
in the summer night.
I'm very fond of fishermen along rivers
and old folks and those who come out after long illnesses.

They have something in their eyes
that the world doesn't see anymore,
old people—like convalescents
who aren't steady enough on their feet yet,
foreheads pale, as after fever.

Old people
who become themselves again slowly
and are slowly dissolved,
like a haze, imperceptibly, they melt
into sleep
and light.

Den omvendte sommeren

Det brenner også en annen sommer på jorden
den omvendte, som vokser nedover i mørket
som speilbildet i de stille sjøene.

Den har hengende trær og hvitt gress,
alt vridd som av hemmelige vinder.

Vet jeg hvor virkeligheten er? Er jeg
rot eller er jeg krone. Er det ikke stjerner
også der, av svakt lysende sten?

The Inverted Summer

There's a second summer burning on the earth—
the inverted one, that grows downward in the dark
like the mirror image in the still lakes.

It has hanging trees and white grass,
all twisted as if by secret winds.

Do I know where reality lies? Am I
root or am I crown. Aren't there stars
there too, made of faintly shining stone?

Midtsommernattens lys

Midtsommernatten er ikke en riktig natt,
det er en galskap i den, en is rundt hjertet
fra en angst ute bak skogene et sted,
noen som vil skrike men kan ikke få frem et ord.

Måltrostens vanviddsfløyte
tørster efter salighet men kan ikke få den.
Lyset er fylt av noen som vil gråte i det,
som har lagt blomstene igjen på marken
og skjuler det hvite ansikt i hendene.

Midtsommernattens lys
skingrer bak skogene og over sjøenes is
som de glitrende øynene på den avsindige,
som steg og steg svimlende gjennem sol
og blomstenes røk, men kjenner først i natt
i denne time i sitt kjøds begjær
at han er av dødens ætt.

Midsummer Night's Light

Midsummer Night isn't a proper night,
there's a lunacy in it, ice around the heart
from a dread deep in the woods somewhere,
someone who wants to scream but can't get a word out.

The song thrush's crazy warble
thirsts for salvation but cannot get it.
The light is full of someone's longing to weep in it,
he's left his flowers behind on the ground
and is hiding his white face in his hands.

The light of Midsummer Night
screeches beyond the woods and across the lake-ice
like the glittering eyes of a madman
who climbed and climbed dizzily through sun
and the flowers' perfúme, but first senses tonight
in this hour in the lust of his flesh
that he is one of death's tribe.

Turnipshøst

Det er tungt dette som vi løfter opp av jorden her
som mursten og marmorpostamenter
efter det store soltemplet til Vitsilopochtli.
Grav mer, her er gudinnens lår
mørke av jord. Bær dem bort.

Turnip Crop

It's heavy, what we lift from the earth here
is heavy as bricks and marble pedestals,
remnants of the great sun-temple of Huitzilopochtli.
Dig more, here are the goddess's thighs
dark with earth. Carry them off.

Mjødurt

Mjødurt, den rykende blomsten
som kommer inn midtveis i sommeren,
lik et hemmelig presteskap med svingende røkelseskar
langs diker og grøft overalt på de grønne marker.

Det er gesantskapet for de kongelige skyene
Cumulus og Nimbus som er vandret ned til Jorden,
at de ikke skal føres nakne gjennem veitene
men mellem prosesjoner
og lys rykende som skyer.

Meadowsweet

Meadowsweet, those dizzying flowers
that arrive midway through summer,
like a secret order swirling their censers
along dips and gullies all over the green fields.

They serve as retinue for the royal clouds
Cumulus and Nimbus, who have descended to the Earth—
so they will not be led through the ditches naked,
but in long processions
with lights swirling like clouds.

Sorgfulle tårn

Slavene hadde veldige hender og bygde sorgfulle tårn.
De hadde hjerter av bly og skuldre som fjellvegger og bygde
   sorgfulle tårn.
De hadde hender som stenhammere og bygde berger av taushet.
De står i Burgund og Baalbek og Xeres de la Frontera.
Askegrå murer over skogene, panner av sten og tungsindige øyne,
mange steder på jorden
hvor svaler går ut i store sløyfer i luften
som lydløse svepeslag.

Mournful Towers

The slaves had powerful hands and built mournful towers.
They had leaden hearts and shoulders like rocky cliffs and built
    mournful towers.
They had hands like boulders and built mountains of silence.
They stand in Burgundy and Baalbek and Jerez de la Frontera.
Ash-gray walls above the forests, foreheads of stone and
    melancholy eyes,
in many places on the earth
where swallows dash out in wide loops in the air
like silent strokes of a whip.

Stavkirker

Jeg tror på de mørke kirkene,
de som ennu står som tjærebål i skogene
og bærer duft med sig som de dyprøde rosene
fra tider som kanskje eide mer kjærlighet.
De sotsvarte tårnene tror jeg på, de som lukter av solbrannen
og gammel røkelse brent inn av seklene.
  Laudate pueri Dominum, laudate nomen Domini.

Øksene teljet dem til og sølvklokker klang i dem.
Noen skar drømmer inn og ga dem vinger å vandre med
ut gjennem tider og fjell. De velter som brottsjø omkring dem.
Nu er de skip, med utkikkstønnene vendt mot Ostindia,
Santa Maria, Pinta og Niña da dagene mørknet
mot verdens ende, årelangt fra Andalusia.
  Laudate pueri Dominum, laudate nomen Domini.

Angst overalt, selv Columbus er redd nu
der hildringer lokker dem frem og vinden har slangetunger.
Stjernene stirrer urørlige ned med avsindige jernøyne,
alle dager er onde, det er ingen redning mer, men vi
seiler, seiler, seiler.
  Laudate pueri Dominum, laudate nomen Domini.

Stave Churches

I believe in the dark churches,
the ones that still stand like tarred pyres in the woods
and like deep red roses carry a fragrance
from times that perhaps had more love.
Those jet-black towers I believe in: the ones that smell of
    the sun's heat
and old incense burnt in by the centuries.
    Laudate pueri Dominum, laudate nomen Domini.

Axes shaped them and silver bells rang in them.
Someone carved dreams in and gave them wings so they'd wander
out across ages and mountains—which surge up around them
    like breakers.
Now they are ships, with crow's nests turned toward East India,
the Santa Maria, Pinta and Niña when the days grew dark
near the end of the world, years out from Andalucía.
    Laudate pueri Dominum, laudate nomen Domini.

Everywhere dread, now fear takes even Columbus
as mirages lure them on and the wind has the tongues of a serpent.
The stars stare down impassively with demented eyes of iron,
every day is evil, there's no hope of being saved, but we
keep sailing, sailing, sailing.
    Laudate pueri Dominum, laudate nomen Domini.

fra SOMMEREN I GRESSET

≈ ≈ ≈ ≈ ≈

1956

from SUMMER IN THE GRASS

≈ ≈ ≈ ≈ ≈

1956

Hånd og munn

Menneskemunnen
er fredeligere enn løvens,
den har hjertets bue over sig
og et lys av blomster
sommetider.

Menneskehånden
har ingen klo som rev og ulv
men har liljens linjer,
en blomst som åpner sig og
lukker sig igjen.

Hand and Mouth

The human mouth
is more peaceful than the lion's,
it has the heart's bow upon it
and a light like flowers
sometimes.

The human hand
has no claw like fox and wolf
but has the lily's lines,
a flower that opens and
closes again.

Månen og apalen

Når apalen blomstrer
kommer ofte månen som en blomst,
blekere enn dem alle
og lyser over treet.

Det er den døde sommeren,
den hvite søsteren til blomstene som kommer igjen
for å se til oss
og lyse fred med sine hender,
at det ikke skal kjennes tungt når ilden kommer.
For Jorden selv er en blomst, sier den,
på stjernenes tre,
blek og med blad
av lysende hav.

The Moon and the Apple Tree

When the wild apple blossoms
often the moon shows up as a flower,
paler than the rest,
and shines above the tree.

It is the dead summer,
the flowers' white sister,
returning to visit
and make peace shine upon us
so the fire to come won't seem too hard.
For the Earth itself is a flower, it says,
on the tree of stars,
pale and with petals
of luminous ocean.

Gamle menns graver

Gamle menns graver
er som ungdommens graver
ganske stille og med solhvite sten,
men det er mere av jord i dem
og dypere ensomheter
i gravene til gamle menn.

Større himmel er det også i dem
og mildere sol eftersom alle ting
vender tilbake til sig selv.
Derfor skulde det stå store trær
med susende kroner hvelvet
over gamle menns graver.

Old Men's Graves

Old men's graves
are like the graves of youth,
quite still and with sun-bleached stones,
but there is more earth in them
and deeper loneliness
in the graves of old men.

There is also bigger sky in them
and milder sun, insofar as all things
turn back into themselves.
Therefore great trees should stand
with rustling crowns vaulted
over old men's graves.

Nattfugl

Kråkene er nattens fugler.
Tungt kommer de ut av demringen
og speider på oss med stenkullsøyne
hele dagen og med hårde skrik,
at vi ikke skal fortape oss i lyset.
Tunge skygger over takene,
mørke vinger på rutene
binder trådene sammen
fra natt til natt.

Nightbird

Crows are the birds of night.
Ponderously, out of the dawn, they come
and guard us with anthracite eyes
all day and with harsh calls,
so we won't lose ourselves in the light.
Heavy shadows over the roofs,
dark wings on the windowpanes
join the threads
from night to night.

—En annen sol

Det er en annen sol
ute bak solen og et annet lys
tvunnet inn i alle stråler.
Den brenner ikke rød, den brenner hvit.

Det er en annen sol
større enn vår et sted bak lyset.
Den glitrer som smeltende sne
i øynene på den vanvittige.

Det er noen som er brent av en annen sol.
De har øyne som sne og stemmer
bak dører av jern
og har lys av et annet lys.

Det som hugger øynene ned til roten
så de ikke kan flytte blikket mere
eller se forbi
som du.

Smertenes sum i verden.
Sorgens sol, den hvite
kvikksølvflammen høyt
over alt lys.

Sol bak solen. Flamme for alt hvitt i verden:
liljene, sneen, visdommen.
Se konvallen i gresset, liljen i skogen
—hvorfor gjemmer den sig under høye trær,
dypt
i skyggen av løv?

—A Second Sun

There is another sun
out behind the sun and another light
twined into every beam.
It doesn't burn red, it burns white.

There is another sun
larger than ours, somewhere behind the light.
It glitters like melting snow
in the eyes of the crazed.

There are some who are burnt by another sun.
They have eyes like snow and voices
behind iron doors
and they shine with another light.

The kind that chops the eyes down to the root
so they can't shift their gaze anymore
or look beyond
like you.

The sum of all the pain in the world.
Sorrow's sun, the white
quicksilver flame high
above all light.

Sun behind the sun. Flame for everything white in the world:
lilies, snow, wisdom.
Look in the woods at the lily of the valley
—why does it hide under tall trees,
deep
in the shade of leaves?

Grønt lys

Dyr som knitrer i skyggen, alle de skjeve,
forvokste i verden, de med bittesmå ben og altfor mange øyne
kan gjemme sig i gresset, derfor er det til,
lydløst og fullt av måneskinn mellem kontinentene.

Jeg har bodd i gresset hos de små som ligner knekket kvist.
Humlene kom fra sine tårn av soleihov som klokker
inn i mitt hjerte med ord av magisk art.
Vindene tok mitt dikt og bredte det ut som støv.

Jeg har bodd i gresset hos Jorden og jeg har hørt den puste
lik et dyr som har gått langt og er tørst efter vannhullene,
og jeg kjente den legge sig ned om kvelden tungt på siden som
    en bøffel
inne i mørket mellem stjernene hvor det er plass.

Vindenes dans og de store løpeildene i gresset husker jeg ofte:
—Skyggebildene av smil i et ansikt som alltid har tilgivelse.
Men hvorfor den har så stor tålmodighet med oss
dypt inne i jernkjernen, det store magnesiumshjertet, det skjønner
    vi ikke på lenge.

For dette har vi glemt, at Jorden er en stjerne av gress,
en frø-planét, rykende av sporer som skyer, fra hav til hav,
et fokk. Frø biter sig fast under brostenene
og mellem bokstavene i mitt dikt, her er de.

Green Light

Creatures that rustle in the shadows, all the crooked
deformed ones in the world, with tiny feet and far too many eyes,
can hide in the grass—that's why it's there,
silent and full of moonlight among the continents.

I have lived in the grass among the small ones that resemble
    broken twigs.
From their towers of cowslip the bumblebees came like bells
into my heart with words of a magic order.
The winds took my poem and spread it out like dust.

I have lived in the grass with the Earth and I have heard it breathe
like an animal that has walked a long way and is thirsting for the
    water holes,
and I felt it lie down heavily on its side in the evening like
    a buffalo,
in the darkness between the stars, where there is room.

The dance of the winds and the great wildfires in the grass I
    remember often:
—the shadow play of smiles on a face that always shows
    forgiveness.
But why it has such great patience with us
deep down in its iron core, its huge magnesium heart, we are far
    from understanding.

For we have forgotten this: that the Earth is a star of grass,
a seed-planet, swirling with spores as with clouds, from sea to sea,
a whirl of them. Seeds take hold under the cobblestones
and between the letters in my poem, here they are.

Fossestøperen

En mann i Norge. Han som
synger bak skogene støtt
og tumler med jern.

Høyt i kløfter
henger han med smiene sine.
Det ryker der.

Klang er over alt
av den usynlige mann.
Han som helder malm i sjø
og gråsten i juvene,
men får det ikke til.

Alltid bak skogene
hører vi hamrene hans, ding—dong.
Men det går opp i luften og blir bare sang av det
og blått lys oppi granbaret
som hos troll.

The Foundryman of Waterfalls

A man in Norway. The one who
constantly sings beyond the forests
and grapples with iron.

High up in crevasses
he hangs with his forges.
It's steamy there.

Everywhere, the sound
of this invisible man.
Who pours ore into the sea
and granite into canyons
but is never done.

Always beyond the forests
we hear his hammer, bing—bong.
But it melts in the air and becomes only song
and blue light up in the spruces
as among the trolls.

Sjøspeilinger

Når vannene er åpne i Norge
kommer fjellene langsomt frem og titter.
De legger sig på kne og stuper hodene nedi,
tett i tett med berg og skogbryn. Se på dem
som polfarere efter syv parafinvintre,
svette i pelsene nu og kåte vasser de uti
mellem skyenes våte selskjær og isbjørnunger
i alle vannenes åpne råk.

Vann nok! Det er ikke en fjellknark noe sted
som ikke kan dyppe trynet i en sjø
og finne en hvit fisk der og leke litt
om sommeren.

Hå. En liten vannknupp vil jeg finne, jeg òg.
Det er godt for tankene, sier yoghien,
å stå på hodet nedi der en stund
og trekke skyene i halen.

Mirror Lakes

When the lakes have thawed in Norway
the mountains come out slowly and peek.
They get down on their knees and plunge their heads in,
crowding hilltops and the edges of forests. See them as
polar explorers after seven winters of kerosene,
randy now and sweating in their furs they slosh out
between the clouds' wet seal-rocks and polar bear cubs
in all the open channels of the lakes.

Water enough! There's not a mountain geezer anywhere
that can't dip his kisser in a lake
and find a white fish there and play a little
in the summertime.

I'm off! I'll find myself a little bud of water too.
It's good for the mind, says the yogi,
to stand on your head down there awhile
and tow the clouds by their tails.

Hvor går gatene hen?

Hvor går gatene hen
når det ikke er noen sporvogner i dem,
bare støv og brente fyrstikker?
De må være her ved slaktehuset
og ved melkebarene hele tiden,
tørre og grå
står de og biter i stakittene
til langt på kveld.

Det er så mange fattige gater i verden
med bare parallelle sten,
fra gassklokkene til slaktehuset
og en kafé med stoler og disk.

Det er gater som har tapt på forhånd
fordi de har for meget cement i hendene
og for tunge hjerter
fra fødselen av.

Where Do the Streets Go?

Where do the streets go
when there aren't any trolleys in them,
only dust and burnt matches?
They have to stay here by the slaughterhouse
and the luncheonettes forever,
dry and gray they
keep chewing on the picket fences
till late in the evening.

There are so many poor streets in the world
with only rows of paving stones,
from the gas-lamps to the slaughterhouse
and a café with a counter and stools.

There are streets that have lost in advance
because they have too much cement in their hands
and hearts too heavy
right from birth.

I land hvor lyset har en annen farve

I land hvor lyset har en annen farve
kan gatens ansikter en kveld forandres
til perler i et langsomt hav av indigo.

Og du må spørre dig—hva speiler dissse
ild-diademer her, og hvilke hender
har strødd dem ut på dette hav i mørket?

In Countries Where the Light Has Another Color

In countries where the light has another color
faces along the street at dusk
can turn to pearls in a slow indigo sea.

And you have to wonder—what do these
glowing tiaras reflect, and whose hands
scattered them across this dark ocean?

Billedhuggeren

Marmorets hvite tårer
drypper over billedhuggerens hender
når han løfter de kolde somrene frem til oss,
stenenes rosenbilder, all flyktet form
henter han ut igjen fra frost—to kvinneskuldre
en pikes bleke skjød, en pande av sorg
tar form igjen og stenene drypper ned
som tårer over hånden alle dager.

Men nettene lenges nu og han hører redd
i sitt eget bryst en hammer slå,
en meisel banke. Hva finner du her for trekk,
tenker han titt. Hva fanger du nu, min Gud,
og hvilke former
løfter du frem av mig med dine hender
når alle splinter, all min frost er falt?

The Sculptor

The marble's white tears
drip over the sculptor's hands
as he lifts the cold summers out for us;
the stones' rosy images, all vanished form
he teases out again from frost—two womanly shoulders
a girl's pale bosom, a forehead of sorrow
take shape again and the stones drip down
like tears over his hand every day.

But the nights lengthen now and frightened he hears
a hammer strike, a chisel tap
in his own breast. What sort of features will you find here,
he often thinks. What are you capturing now, oh Lord,
and what forms
will you lift out of me with your hands
when all the shards, all my frost has fallen?

I gobelinsalen

Ignazius og Bonaventura, de høye gobeliner
med sitt lys av gammelt sølv og fordervelse,
jeg skulde gjerne bo i dem et århundre
blandt kyrassene der, med maven full av høyfrø,
det kunde kanskje dempe min ærgjerrighet
som har bragt mig helt til Venezia.

For hva skal vi gripe til, vi som leker med støv
når alle de gamle låvene er borte
og alle somrene i dem, de som sovnet med hånd under kinn der
og alle duftene omkring sig som lysstripen over et solefall.

Men i dette høygulvet kan vi leve sølvgrå
i de store bingene her hos Ignazius og Bonaventura,
de er falmet litt mellem hellebardene
men dufter vilt ennå
av Timian og Botticelli. Europas låve
med all den spøkelsesaktige herlighet som stiger opp av
gammel urett.

Her løfter Roland hornet mellem fjellene,
bare som en duft nu og tre tråder med ull,
men jeg har en fløyte her som bare fuglene kan skjønne
og nu kaller jeg dem ned fra skogene som Franciscus,
se, de setter sig rundt mig i lyttende ringer når jeg spiller for dem
om vindenes lek og de grønne skyggene i gresset
til jeg sender dem tilbake igjen til skogene av støv.

La mig da få komme inn i gobelinet
og legge min vindfløyte ned mellem skyggene der,
så spiller den sakte de bleke trådene av tid
til kløverknekt og rosmarin, en dis om skuldrene.
Jeg som likte så godt å velte rundt i gammel kløver,
la mig få gå på hodet inn
i høstens herlighet en gang til
med ansiktet i fioler.

In the Hall of Gobelin Tapestries

Ignatius and Bonaventure, the great Gobelins
with their sheen of old silver and ruin—
I'd gladly live in them a century
among the cuirasses, with my belly full of hayseed;
perhaps that would subdue my ambition,
which has brought me all the way to Venice.

For what shall we fall back on, we who must play with dust,
when all the old barns are gone
and all the summers in them, those who fell asleep there with hand
    under cheek
and all the odors around them like the shaft of light above a sunset.

But in this hayloft we can live, silver-gray,
in the huge bins here at Ignatius and Bonaventure's;
they have faded a bit between the halberds
but still smell of wild
thyme and Botticelli. Europe's barn
with all the ghostly glory that rises up from
ancient injustice.

Here Roland lifts his horn among the mountains,
barely a scent now and three woollen threads,
but I have a flute that only the birds can understand
and now I'm calling them down from the forests like St. Francis—
look, they settle around me in circles and listen while I play
    for them
about the frolic of wind and the green shadows in grass,
until I send them back again to the forests of dust.

Let me come into the Gobelin, then,
and lay my wind-flute down among the shadows,
where it will slowly play the pale threads of time
to rosemary and garlanded knave, a mist about their shoulders.
I who liked so much to roll around in old clover,
let me enter autumn's splendor once more,
head first,
my face in the violets.

fra BREV TIL LYSET

≈ ≈ ≈ ≈ ≈

1960

from LETTER TO THE LIGHT

≋ ≋ ≋ ≋ ≋

1960

Brev til lyset

Morgenens papir er veldig foldet ut
på jorden, det er en ny dag
og en traktor som alt er fremme med sin klumpete neve
og skriver et brev til lyset, hver bokstav
brummer den høyt for seg selv, for det har meget å si
at alt kommer med, både tordnen og biene,
maurveien som har strukket ut sin lille
silkefot i gresset, vår fred
og den uro vi har med alt, skal den ha med.

Store fuktige linjer og en langsom hånd
som ryster svært men nu er alt sagt,
siden er full og alt legges åpent frem
som et brev til ingen, plogenes brev
til lyset som den kan lese som vil.

Letter to the Light

Morning's paper is splendidly unfolded
on the Earth, it is a new day
and a tractor is already out there with its lumpy fist,
writing a letter to the light, growling
each letter aloud to itself, for it's important
to get everything in, the thunder and the bees,
the ant trail that's extended its little
silken foot in the grass, our peace
and the unease we feel about everything—it has to get
all these in.

Large moist lines and a slow hand
that shakes a lot but now it's all said,
the page is full and everything's laid out in the open
like a letter to no-one, the plow's letter
to light that anyone's welcome to read.

I januar

O alt hva du kan i januar
når alle dagene bare rekker deg til knes
og du går døgnet rundt og støter panden mot stjernene
som på et loft med gamle uniformer.
I januar da verden er full til overmål av levende sne
som møter deg med glade bjeff mot ruten
og legger seg lydig ned foran alle dører ut
som en stor vennlig hund
som kommer med tungen og vil slikke deg skarpt på hendene.

I januar
når alt er stengt og alle veier muret med cement
og du kan gå ut og lage huller i den med begge ben
og gjøre nesten alt. Gå ut eller være i ro,
rydde en skuff
og finne sky og meget unge billeder der
som du kan brenne—eller vente litt.

Og ta en bok i hånden, blåse litt støv
og bøye bladene tilbake i sin ro
som lette snefall. Brev
med stive skrifter, håndtrykk
over havet der vi kom fra, hit
til landet uten lyd
hvor alt er ens og alle ansikter er flate
som tallskivene på ur, de trekker øyenbrynet opp
når du har tenkt en utålmodig tanke.

Hva kan du mer i januar,
når alle ord er snakket døde
og ligger strødd omkring som krøllete aviser
og alle sår er bundet om med gaze
og alle spor er vasket bort
og du kan gå rundt og høre plankene knirke
og ovnene knurre rolig over sine kjøttben.

≈

In January

O the slew of things you can do in January
when the days come no higher than your knees
and you keep bumping your head against the stars day and night
as in an attic full of old uniforms.
In January when the world is overflowing with live snow
that meets you with happy barks against the windowpane
and lies down obediently outside all the doors
like a big friendly dog
that comes over with its tongue out and wants to lick you roughly
   on the hands.

In January
when everything's closed and all the roads have walls of cement
and you can go out and make holes in it with both feet
and do almost anything. Go out or stay in,
tidy up a drawer
and find shy and very young pictures there
that you can burn—or wait a bit.

And take up a book, blow off some dust
and thumb the pages back to rest
like a light snowfall. Letters
with stiff writing, hands touching
across the ocean where we came from, to this
land without sound
where everything's the same and all faces are flat
as the faces of clocks, they raise their eyebrows
when you've thought an impatient thought.

What more can you do in January,
when all words are talked to death
and lie strewn about like curled-up newspapers
and all wounds are bound up with gauze
and all tracks are blotted out
and you can walk around and hear the floorboards creaking
and the heaters softly growling over their meat-bones.

≈

—Sett deg. Legg ut din store kabal
som aldri går opp og spør
hva du kan gjøre for ditt hjerte mere enn det.
By det en mørkere tobakk? Klyve opp på en stige
og heise en drabelig røk som et flagg opp fra din skorsten
til glede for skyene som kommer drivende nu fra Karelen
med underlige forrevne bryst,
for å ruge de nye dager ut
og den lille gule sol du snart får se
på gjerdestolpene i februar.

Men nu i januar—da skal du vente på ditt hjerte.
La stjernene bare klirre ved din seng. Du ser
en pande komme frem, et ansikt i nordlyset.
Bak blygrå gardiner setter hun frem sin lave lampe
ved puten din så hun kan se på deg
om dine trekk er blitt forandret.

—Sit down. Lay out your great game of solitaire
that never works out and ask
what more you can do for your heart than that.
Offer it a darker tobacco? Climb a ladder and raise
a bold flag of smoke from your chimney
to delight the clouds that come driving in now from Karelia
with strangely ragged breasts
to hatch the new days
and the little yellow sun you'll soon see
on the fenceposts in February.

But now in January—now you must wait for your heart.
Let the stars go on rattling by your bed. You see
a forehead emerging, a face in the northern lights.
Behind lead-gray curtains she sets her dim lamp out
near your pillow so she can see
if your features have been changed.

Nattvindu

Et vindu mot natten og isnende høyt der ute
ser jeg en stjerne stå som en ørn i skyer
ute ved verdens grense der alle rop forstummer.
Kanskje den venter på mitt hjerte nu eller en annens,
men vindushaspene er på og nattens møll vil inn
med tusen hender og gripe fatt i mitt lys
som den druknendes rop, men det forgår,
vingene knuses og alle er døde snart.
Det store farveslam efter solen er vasket ut
og natten høy og stum, jeg hører
ditt rolige åndedrett der du går omkring i søvnens hus,
de store rum hvor jeg ikke kan komme inn.
Du flytter på ting som er kommet ut av sin fred,
rydder i skap og på bord og jeg kan merke
ditt ansikt derinne, din pande bak gardinet
med forandrede trekk og øyne jeg ikke kjenner.

Men hånden er ikke med, den ligger ute
på teppet som din lille vakthund, halvt sovende
halvt våken og det ene øret løftet opp
mot mine tanker.

Nu er den tredje time da alt levende er kommet i hus
og stjernene kommer ned for å holde råd på jorden,
med stenharde øyne, ubevegelige som fugler
står de i ring om våre hus som ved et tingsted
og dømmer til døden eller til livet det som er hendt
og det som skal skje i morgen legges klart for alle.

Men din pust er rolig som en isnende kilde
hvor tankene sildrer nesten lydløst forbi mot elven
over røtter og de lave stener i din drøm
hvor skyggeaktige fisk står snute mot snute sovende
med vidåpne øyne bak de store grå-hellere der,
eller i de klare hvelv på bunden. Det er en gate mot havet

Night Window

A window on the night and freezing high out there
I see a star hanging among clouds like an eagle,
out at the border of the world where all cries die down.
Perhaps it's waiting for my heart now, or another's,
but the window hasps are latched and the night-moths want
    to come in
with a thousand hands and grab hold of my light
like a drowning man's cry; but it passes,
their wings are broken and soon they'll all be dead.
The slush of color spread by the sun is washed out
and the night high and still, I hear
your steady breathing as you walk around in sleep's house,
the large rooms I cannot enter.
You shift things that have been disturbed,
tidy up closets and tables and I can make out
your face in there, your forehead behind the curtain,
with changed features and eyes I don't know.

But your hand hasn't joined in, it's lying outside
on the blanket, your little watchdog, half asleep
half awake with one ear pricked up
toward my thoughts.

Now is the third hour, when all living things are safe at home
and the stars come down to hold council on Earth;
with eyes hard as stone, unmoving as birds
they stand around our house in circles as at an ancient moot
and sentence—to death or to life—what has happened,
and what must happen tomorrow is made plain to everyone.

But your breathing is quiet as an ice-cold spring,
where the thoughts trickle by almost soundlessly toward the river
across roots and the low rocks in your dream
where shadowlike fish hang sleeping snout to snout
with wide-open eyes behind large blocks of slate,
or in the clear vaults at the bottom. It's a street to the sea

der jeg er bregnen og den lave hyldegren
som fanger inn sitt disige billede her
hvor ingen krusning ennå gjør linjene forandret
og kanskje en stjernes stål forviller seg også dit.
Som en ørn med glitrende nebb venter den på mine øyne.

and I am the ferns and the low elder-branch
that take in their foggy picture
where there's no rippling yet to change the lines,
and perhaps the blade of a star will go astray here too.
Like an eagle with glistening beak it waits for my eyes.

Blind sang

Billedavtrykket efter sten
som har ligget lenge i jorden,
ligner det ikke ansikter som har grått,
de blinde stedene i hjertet
når frykten er tatt bort.
Kribledyret piler ut, mauren blusser opp som en rødme.

Disse avtrykk efter sten,
se hvor de ligner sorg,
ansikter uten form
nesten forblødd
i Tidens fotefar
under støvlene til en
som setter foten langsomt ned
fra vår til høst,
han som går lydløst gjennem skogene
og har god tid til alt.

Han løfter bergene ned
og sender skyene foran seg i prosesjoner
til helt andre steder på jorden
hvor de faller ned som sne, som sne.

Han vender tålmodig den venstre kinn mot solen
når den rammer ham på hans høyre.
Han henter dine hender inn til ro
og de små barn til søvn.
Han kaller sporvognene hjem fra sine gater
og de små papegøyer til sine hus av bittert løv.
Bare stjernene kan han ikke rope hjem
når han står ute på store fjell for å se efter dem.
De går forbi med sine rykende fakler
lik en krigshær som er ute for å lete efter en fiende
som har gjemt seg langt borte i et tårn
eller i de mørke kløftene i fjell.

≈

Blind Song

The pictures pressed into the earth
by stones that have lain there for ages—
don't they look like faces that have been weeping,
the blind places left in the heart
when fear is removed.
Bugs and worms rush out, the ants flare up like a blush.

These impressions left by stones—
how they resemble sorrow,
faces without form
almost drained of blood
in the footprints of Time
under the boots of someone
who sets his foot down slowly
from spring to fall,
someone who goes silently through the woods
and has plenty of time.

He reaches up to bring down the mountains
and sends the clouds before him in procession
to other, distant places on the earth
where they fall as snow, as snow.

He turns his left cheek patiently toward the sun
when it strikes him on the right one.
He calls your hands to their rest
and the little children to their sleep.
He calls trolley cars home from their streets
and small parrots into their houses of bitter leaves.
The stars are all that he cannot call home
as he stands on high mountains to wait for them.
They pass by with their smoldering torches
like an army at war out hunting an enemy
that has hidden far away in a tower
or in dark mountain crevasses.

≈

De store bevegelser i ditt liv,
stener som flyttes om. Død uten håp
eller oppstandelse uten trøst.
Se den kjolekledde pianist i sin sal av hissende marmor
når han setter seg ned bak flyglets mørke vinge
hvordan han bøyer hodet langsomt som i bønn,
hendene løftes, fingrene beveger seg
som svaners nakker, en besvergelse
til tonen bryter ut, et maestoso
fyller hvelvene med ord
som ikke er av mennesket,
mørkt lysende, strenge og tause ord,
seierrike, hemmelighetsfulle ord,
latter fra en stjerne, sang fra en gud med leber av krystall
og du skal gå ut og gråte lenge
for du har enda meget du skal elske.

Eller når du hører maskingeværene i den brennende storbyen
på demonenes dag
når gatekampene er forbi og de siste liv blåses ut
mot kjellerveggene med håndgranater
—slik—og slik—og slik. Det er nok
og du kan gjemme ditt ansikt under en helle. Dekke over deg
    med sten.

Bonden går i hverdagen
og vet noe
som ikke vi vet.
Han har en hemmelighet sammen med plogfuren
og vinterfrosten og den dumpe skyggen under trær
som han holder inne med
for det kan være det samme.
Treet drikker sin stumhet av jorden,
det setter sin svære rot som en snabel dypt derned
og drikker taushet der
og løfter den opp til stjernene og til vinden

The great shifts in your life,
stones being moved around. Death without hope
or resurrection without relief.
Look at the pianist in tails in his hall of rousing marble
as he seats himself behind the instrument's black wing,
how he bows his head slowly as if in prayer,
the hands are raised, the fingers move
like the necks of swans, a conjuring
until the notes break out, a maestoso
fills the vaulted roof with words
that are not those of humans,
darkly shining, strict and silent words,
triumphant, mysterious words,
laughter from a star, song from a god with lips of crystal
and you will go out and weep a long while
for there is still much for you to love.

Or when you hear machine guns in the burning city
on the day of demons
when the street battles are over and the last lives are being
    blown out
against cellar walls with hand grenades
—like this—and this—and this. That's enough
and you can hide your face under a boulder. Cover yourself
    with stone.

The farmer in his everyday life
knows something
that we don't know.
He has a secret with the plow's furrow
and the winter frost and the dull shade under trees,
a secret that he keeps
because it's just as well.
The tree drinks its muteness from the earth,
extends its enormous root down there like an elephant trunk
and draws up silence
and lifts it to the stars and the wind

at de skal smake alle.
De døde i gravene taler ikke meget.
Kanskje det er tausheten som betyr noe.
Kanskje det er derfor diktets munn
har den laveste av alle jordens stemmer,
nesten som gresset
eller som sangen under en sten.
Hva skal vi tro.
Kribledyret piler bort. Mauren blusser opp som en rose.

so they can taste it too.
The dead in their graves don't talk much.
Maybe silence is what means something.
Maybe that's why the poem's mouth
has the softest of voices,
almost like the grass
or the song under a stone.
Who can say.
Bugs and worms rush out. The ants flare up like a rose.

Nu bærer elven sine lamper ut

Nu bærer elven sine lamper ut.
Stenbildet dypt i bekker
som vannets hender lenge ville skjule,
trer rolig frem som skår av keramikk

der pander av kisel bøyes mot kalkstensskuldre
og viser oss klart at ingenting skal vare
mer enn en hastig tid, et åndedrett mot kinnet,
et streif av flyktende leber nu før lampene bæres ut

og stenbildet kommer frem i de tørre bekker
som brune skår og skall av knuste vaser.
De var av ler, de var for spinkelt bygget
for denne sols umåtelige ild.

Now the River Is Carrying Off Its Lights

Now the river is carrying off its lights.
The stone-picture deep in streams,
shielded so long by hands of water,
calmly appears as pottery shards

where silica foreheads lean toward limestone shoulders
and show us clearly that nothing will endure
more than a brief time, a breath on the cheek,
a touch of fleeting lips now before the lights are carried off

and the stone-picture appears in the dry streams
as brown shards and the shells of broken vases.
They were of clay, they were too fragile
for this sun's intense fire.

Minnet om hester

Linjene i de gamles hender
bøyer seg langsomt og peker snart mot jorden.
Dit tar de med sitt hemmelige sprog,
skyenes ord og vindenes bokstaver,
alle de tegn som hjertet samler opp i armodens år.

Sorg blekes ut og vender seg til stjernene
men minnet om hester, kvinneføtter, barn
strømmer fra deres ansikter over i gressets rike.

I store trær kan vi ofte se
billeder av dyreflankers ro,
og vinden tegner i gresset, hvis du er glad,
løpende barn og hester.

The Memory of Horses

The lines in old people's hands
bend over slowly and soon point toward the earth.
They take their secret language there with them,
words from the clouds and letters from the winds,
all the signs the heart stores up in the meager years.

Sorrow bleaches out and turns to the stars
but the memory of horses, women's feet, children
streams from their faces into the grass's kingdom.

In large trees we can often picture
the calm of animal flanks,
and the wind draws in the grass, if you are happy,
running children and horses.

Små lys på havet

Din hånd som hviler her, er en hvelvet båt
halvt trukket opp på stranden
og full av åndedrag som en konkylie
venter den på deg at du skal komme tilbake.

Og jeg kan se at enda er noen ute
på havet som snart er helt mørkt nu
—fiskere som har tent lys i båter
som bølgeryggene langsomt løfter opp
og langsomt ned igjen som om de lette
med lamper, myggefine foran et mektig lerret
om de kan finne ut av den ubegripelige signatur
eller lyse et ansikt frem,
en farve som gir håp.

Small Lights at Sea

Your hand at rest is an upturned boat
pulled halfway onto the beach,
and full of breathing as a conch's shell
it waits for you to come back.

And I can see that someone is still out
on the ocean that will be completely dark soon
—fishermen who've turned on lights in boats
that the crests of waves bear slowly up
and slowly down again as if they were searching
with lamps, small as gnats before a great canvas,
to make out the undecipherable signature
or bring to light a face,
a color that offers hope.

Gamle ur

Gamle ur har ofte vennlige ansikter
og kan minne om bønder fra skogbygder og fjell
med en rolig likesælhet i sitt vesen
som om de hørte til en annen slekt enn vår

som kanskje har stridd ut sin tid hernede
og sett sin uro visne ned som gresset
i sine store skar og stille myrstrøk
forrige gang Jorden var til.

Nu er de gjester her og nikker til vår kummer
med lavmælt visdom ved vår seng: Det går,
ja, ja, det går, det går.

Old Clocks

Old clocks often have friendly faces
and can remind us of woodcutters and mountain folk,
a calm disinterest in their bearing
as if they belonged to a different race from ours

who perhaps struggled through their time down here
and watched their uneasiness wither away like grass
in great chasms and still marshlands
the last time Earth existed.

Now they are visitors here and nod to our sadness
with low-voiced wisdom by our bed: It's all right,
just fine, all right, all right.

Tausheten i trær

Om natten når de små orkestre reiser hjem
og alle trommene er trette av å tromme
står høye trær langs gatene som porter
av lydløshet, som høye kandelabre
foran et gotisk univers vi ikke fatter.
De gylne saksofonene blir pakket ned
som baby-dolls på rosa silkeputer
—bildører slår igjen med korte smell
og drosjer piler bort i øst og syd
—den store tuba surres fast på taket
som en dukke-elefant med store ører
og klovnen reiser hjem
og sangeren med det store kalciumsmil
og Clarissa, nakendanserinnen, reiser hjem
for å kle av sitt hjerte foran søvnens ansikt,
hver sigarettglo lukker trett sitt øye
og alt blir slettet ut av nattens tavle
med lydløs hånd
så tausheten i trær skal komme frem.

For snart skal alle lyd i verden hjem og sove
og alle farvene bli trette av å farve
og reise bort fra oss til ukjent sted
og alt skal viskes ut med myke kluter
som nu inatt med det støvfine regn som sølv
over alle parker ruvende som porter
inn til et rike vi engang dro bort fra
og tausheten skal bryte frem
i alle trær.

The Silence in Trees

At night when the small ensembles head home
and all the drums are tired of drumming,
tall trees stand along the streets like gates
of soundlessness, like high candelabras
before a Gothic universe we cannot grasp.
The golden saxophones are packed away
like dolls on pink silk cushions
—car doors slam shut with brief bangs
and taxis dart away to east and south
—the big tuba is lashed down on the roof
like a toy elephant with huge ears
and the clown goes home
and the singer with the big calcium smile,
and Clarissa, the nude dancer, goes home
to unclothe her heart before the face of sleep,
each cigarette glow tiredly shuts its eye
and everything's wiped off the slate of night
by a soundless hand
so the silence of trees will come out.

For soon all the sounds in the world will go home to sleep
and all the colors will get tired of coloring
and travel away from us to who knows where
and everything will be rubbed out by soft cloths
as now, tonight, by powdered-silver rain
over all the parks looming like gates
to a kingdom we once left behind
and the silence will break out
in all the trees.

Glassoldater

Hårdt regn om dagene
minner om soldater, det har rå hender
og striper av gjørmet vann i øynene.

Det går på tusen føtter gjennem Europas byer,
som vegger av stål, loddrett med bajonettene på,
spisse trommer og fløyter,
fanene gråflammet av å ha ligget forlenge i jorden

—uten betydning for de har ingen ansikter,
bare føtter og hender, føtter og hender i all evighet
forbi de lunkne i alle portene,—de stymperaktige
forbannede overlevende fra alle kriger.

Europas regn, halvvarmt, tusenårig
som blod i ansiktet, søle i øynene,
druenes tårer, valmuens røde munn.

Glass Soldiers

These days hard rain
recalls soldiers; it has raw hands
and streaks of muddy water in its eyes.

It moves on a thousand feet through Europe's cities,
like walls of steel, bolt upright with bayonets fixed,
sharp fifes and drums,
banners veined with gray from lying too long in the earth

—all the same to them, since they have no faces,
only feet and hands, feet and hands forever
passing lukewarm people in every doorway: the miserable
damned survivors of all our wars.

Europe's tepid rain, as eternal
as blood in the face, mire in the eyes,
the vineyard's musty tears,
the poppy's red mouth.

Tårnene i Bologna

Tårnene i Bologna, de to
som bare står og står i en luft av sølv
og luter seg nesten umerkelig mot hverandre
fordi de er trette av tiden og stjernenes tog ustanselig.

De strekker langsomt sine skygger ut mot verden
for å prøve forsiktig hvor langt all tid er kommet,
kjenner på torvenes blå druer og solpikenes bryst om de er hårde
og føler seg sakte frem langs alle murers revner
til tårnenes flaggermus, og kirkeklokkenes malm.

Blått regn kommer og svinger milde flagg over deres ansikter
—den store lombardiske fane og syv bannere
fra Piacenza og Modena, men de husker dem ikke lenger.
Alt er kommet så langt ut og de er nesten blinde
i et land hvor solen knurrer som en tiger mot alle
og fyller våre lunger helt tilbunds med truslen om sønderrivelse,
der morgenen kommer og strør sitt fattige salt på fortauene
og piker med brune kinn kommer ned i portene
nesten opphovnet i munnen av for meget natt.

Asinelli og Garisenda, de to
hellende tårn som går rundt over byen med sine skygger
som et slags langsomt ur med sine visere
for timene av elskov og forferdelse, hva sier tiden,
hvor langt er det kommet med alle.

Hver dag må de se
damen i porselensbutikken som tørrer støv med silkekluter
hvor de små bjeller har spinkle lyd som sølv
og de ser bussjåførene som går bort og røker cigar i skyggen
    av sine tårn,
mødre som gir småbarn bryst i dem,
og gamle ektefolk som kan hate hverandre i mørket fra disse tårn,

The Towers in Bologna

The towers in Bologna, those two
that just stand and stand in silver air
and lean almost imperceptibly toward each other
because they are tired of time and the stars' constant procession.

Slowly they stretch their shadows out toward the world,
carefully testing how far time has come,
touch the markets' blue grapes and the sunshine girls' breasts to
    see if they're firm
and feel their way slowly forward along the cracks in all the walls
to the bats in the towers, and the brass of the church bells.

Blue rain comes and swings soft flags above their faces
—the large banner of Lombardy and seven pennants
from Piacenza and Modena—but they don't remember them
    anymore.
Everything's come such a long way and they are almost blind
in a land where the sun growls at everyone like a tiger
and fills our lungs to the bottom with the threat of
    dismemberment,
where morning comes and sprinkles its poor salt on the pavements
and girls with brown cheeks come down into the doorways
with mouths almost swollen by too much night.

Asinelli and Garisenda, those two
leaning towers that sweep across the city with their shadows
like a kind of slow clock with its hands pointing
to the hour for embrace or desolation: What does time say,
how far gone are things for everyone.

Every day they have to see
the lady in the china shop who dusts with scraps of silk
where the little bells have fragile sounds like silver
and they see the bus drivers who go off and smoke cigars in the
    shadows of their towers,
mothers who nurse their babies in them,
and old husbands and wives who can hate each other in the dark
    of these towers,

de springende og jagende som kan være nervøse i dem,
slakteren som hugger opp sine koteletter,
prestene som leser sitt officium
i skyggene fra Asinelli og Garisenda
evighetens tårn, litt trette av å være
mann og kvinne, dag og natt, og vise
altets dobbelte natur, det tvedelte liv
som lengter efter forening
som de store trær lengter efter aftnen i skogen
og den store endeløse stjerne.

the hurriers and scurriers who can be nervous in them,
the butcher slicing his pork chops,
the priests reading their Office
in the shadows of Asinelli and Garisenda,
eternity's towers, a bit tired of being
man and woman, day and night, of showing
the duality of the universe, the divided life
that longs for union
as the great trees long for evening in the forest
and that large, enduring star.

Katakombene i San Callisto

En by i døden med gatene styrtet inn og trafikklysene stumme.

En by sett i et knust speil som vi må gni mørket av med hendene.

Under stjernene og under jorden, en by som en latter bak
en lukket dør.

Et Venezia av natt, broer som speiler seg i støv.

Verdens stolthet, en by med panden kløvet og ansiktet grodd ned
med slam.

Tynne rottrevler som fingre og føtter, hender og skulderblad av
skjeletter.

Røtter og grener av røtter, døde som bøyer fingrene om mørket
som rundt en sten.

Et tre opp av vår knuste virkelighet med roten plantet i fornedrelse.

Et tre som strekker grenene ut over jorden og rekker nesten til
stjernene, Arcturus, Capella.

Et tre fra jordens hjerte. Forundring. Trofasthet.

The Catacombs of San Callisto

A city in death with its streets caved in and traffic lights still.

A city seen in a broken mirror we have to rub the darkness from with our hands.

Beneath the stars and beneath the earth, a city like a laugh behind a closed door.

A Venice of night, bridges reflected in dust.

The pride of the world, a city with its forehead split open and its face overgrown with slime.

Thin shreds of root like fingers and feet, hands and shoulder blades of skeletons.

Roots and branches of roots, dead that bend their fingers around the dark as around a stone.

A tree up from our broken reality, with its root planted in humiliation.

A tree that stretches its branches out over the earth and reaches almost to the stars, Arcturus, Capella.

A tree from the earth's heart. Wondrous. Keeping faith.

fra Stillheten efterpå— — —

≈ ≈ ≈ ≈ ≈

1965

from THE SILENCE AFTERWARDS — — —

≈ ≈ ≈ ≈ ≈

1965

Langsomt— —

Bilder av umåtelige land,
sandflukter, bronceaktige himler
skal stå til tidenes ende, vinden
løfter det lille sandkornet opp på en sten,
regnværet skyller det bort.

Således er jordens ansikt mellem stjernebildene
dekket av glemsel—langsom
som stenene er Guds gjøren med oss,
en dag skal komme som en rose—en dag som en ild.
Alt har sin tid.
Om tusen år
er sneglen kommet frem til treet.

Jeg ser et gammelt regnvær gå bøyd over aftenens land
og lete med tynne hender efter de glemte ting,
det ingen enser mer—stillheten mellem strå,
halvsagte ord, bruddstykker av fortapthet, tanker
nesten ingen har tenkt, de tause
veier av gress og søvn som fører frem
fra tid til tid.

Hvor finner vi nu
det som kan binde sammen det spredte.
Stien i stjernene, kompassnålens veier
eller linjene i alle pikers hender
som ligner vinden gjennem rosene.
For det er sent

snart bærer elven mine bilder ut,
åssider, speilinger av hus, et elsket ansikt
bærer den ut til havet. Alt skal ryddes
uten et ord og kloden bøyer
rolig sin skulder mot natt og dag.
Et sted suser vinden alt morgenen inn i skogene,
et sted går omrisset av en bergvegg umerkelig inn i natten.

Slowly— —

Images of measureless lands,
sand dunes, bronzelike skies
will last till the eons end; the wind
lifts the little sand-grain onto a stone,
rain washes it away.

This is how the earth's face among the constellations
is covered by forgetfulness—slowly:
God's dealings with us are as slow as the stones.
One day will come like a rose—one day like a flame;
everything has its time.
In a thousand years
the snail will have reached the tree.

I see ancient rain walking bent across evening's land
and searching with thin hands for the forgotten things,
what no one notices anymore—the stillness between blades
    of grass,
half-uttered words, fragments of loss, thoughts
almost no one has thought, the silent
roads of grass and sleep that lead forward
from age to age.

Where do we find now
a way to connect what is scattered.
The trail in the stars, the compass needle's course
or the lines in girls' hands
that are like the wind through the roses.
For it is late

soon the river will carry off my images;
hillsides, reflections of houses, a beloved face—
it will carry them out to sea. Everything will be cleared off
without a word and the planet will calmly
turn its shoulder toward night and day.
Somewhere the wind is already rushing morning into the forests,
somewhere the outline of a rocky cliff passes gradually into night.

Stillheten efterpå

Prøv å bli ferdige nu
med provokasjonene og salgsstatistikkene,
søndagsfrokostene og forbrenningsovnene,
militærparadene, arkitektkonkurransene
og de tredobbelte rekkene med trafikklys.
Kom igjennem det og bli ferdige
med festforberedelser og markedsføringsanalyser
for det er sent,
det er altfor sent,
bli ferdige og kom hjem
til stillheten efterpå
som møter deg som et varmt blodsprøyt mot panden
og som tordenen underveis
og som slag av mektige klokker
som får trommehindene til å dirre
for ordene er ikke mere til,
det er ikke flere ord,
fra nu av skal alt tale
med stemmene til sten og trær.

Stillheten som bor i gresset
på undersiden av hvert strå
og i det blå mellemrommet mellem stenene.
Stillheten
som følger efter skuddene og efter fuglesangen.
Stillheten
som legger teppet over den døde
og som venter i trappene til alle er gått.
Stillheten
som legger seg som en fugleunge mellem dine hender,
din eneste venn.

The Silence Afterwards

Try to be done now
with the challenges and the sales statistics,
the Sunday brunches and the combustion furnaces,
the military parades, the architectural competitions
and the six lanes with traffic lights.
Come through that and be done
with party preparations and market-research analyses,
for it is late,
it is much too late,
be done and come home
to the silence afterwards
that meets you like a warm spurt of blood against your forehead
and like thunder rolling
and like strokes of mighty bells
that set your eardrums quivering,
for words don't exist anymore,
there are no more words,
from now on everything will speak
with the voices of stone and tree.

The silence that lives in the grass
on the underside of each blade
and in the blue space between the stones.
The silence
that follows the shots and the birdsong.
The silence
that lays a blanket over someone who's died
and that waits in the stairwell till everyone's left.
The silence
that rests like a baby bird between your hands,
your only friend.

Nattemørket

Nattemørket overlever i krokene
mellem gulvbjelkene og i stengte skap
til det skal bre seg ut over verden.
Vi pisker natten med våre lys,
neon og ildkaskader over gatene
og driver det ut i skogene og ned i gresset.
Men det kommer igjen
i våre hjerter, inne mellem fryktens bjelker,
nede i uvisshetens gress
venter det på timen da det skal slå ut sin mørke vinge
fra Sirius og til bunden av det siste hav.

The Dark of Night

The dark of night survives in the nooks
between floor beams and in closed closets
until it's time to spread out over the world.
We pelt the night with our lights,
neon and fiery cascades across the streets,
and drive it out into the woods and down into the grass.
But it comes back
in our hearts; inside, between the timbers of fear,
down in the grass of uncertainty
it waits for the hour when it will spread its dark wing
from Sirius to the bottom of the last ocean.

Tanker ved avlytting av et radioteleskop

Da radioen sendte lydopptak av stjernestøyen
fra universet CO-35m i Centauren, verdens ytterste
kom visergutten inn med varene fra kjøpmannen
—Det er no galt med apparatet Deres, hører jeg.

Noe galt med apparatet. Jo vi kan høre
verden brenne der ute, men det er flammer av kulde
fra dommedager lenger ute enn døden
som falmet til støv endog før lyset fødtes.

Og eldre enn Sagenetrikken, ufattbare tiders
vandringer er endt i denne lenestol på en torsdag
like før pinse med lokaltoget syv minutter forsinket,
køer i butikkene og en skurring i apparatet

der stjernen vedblir å tale med støtvise ord og hutrende
bruddstykkevis fra de dødes rike til de levendes
men kablene er sprengt og vi forstår ikke
tid eller sted for noe er hendt med oss,

og vi famler i blinde. Dette
er kyster vi aldri har sett, kanskje tidsaldre
bak mørkets teppe, dimensjoner
like ved vårt ansikt som kan forandre alt.

Kanskje et ekko av oss selv, konkyliesuset av våre kriger
eller bølgeslagene fra et hav under menneskets hjerte.
—Hva skal vi tro.

Seil spennes ut i natten—våre dømmer,
ukjente skip går forbi
på hav ingen kan se.

Thoughts upon Listening In on a Radio Telescope

As the radio was broadcasting a tape of the noise of stars
from Galaxy CO-35m in Centaurus, the most distant known,
the delivery boy came in with packages from the grocer
—There's somethin' wrong with your set, sounds like.

Something wrong with the set. Not quite: We can hear
the world burning out there, but it is flames of cold
from doomsdays further out than death
that faded to dust even before the light was born.

And older than the Sagene trolley, wanderings through
inconceivable ages have ended in this easy chair on a Thursday
just before Pentecost with the local train seven minutes late,
lines in the shops and a burring on the set

where the star goes on with its shivering words,
speaking in snatches from the realm of the dead to the living
but the cables are overloaded and we cannot understand
time or place, for something has happened to us

and we grope blindly. These
are coasts we have never seen, perhaps eons
behind the curtain of darkness, or in dimensions
just beside our face that can change everything.

Perhaps an echo of ourselves, the conch-shell rush of our wars
or the wash of waves from an ocean under the human heart.
—What are we to think.

Sails are unfurled in the night—our dreams;
unknown ships go by
on oceans no one can see.

Tankeløs—

Inne i alle dager er det et lite hjerte
og en åpen hånd.
Kanskje hver dag er et liv for seg.
Morgenen har sin lov og aftenen har sin
og om natten er det en krone av ild over vårt hus
ingen kan nå.

Sommerbekkens lille hvite pande
er full av tanker den ikke kan holde fast på
og hører til i en annen verden, krystallren
men flyktigere, alltid musikk.

Grankonglen faller ned som et gongongslag
og noen netter er fulle av et bronceaktig lys.
Ørreten vandrer i sin elv som et spor
av fruktbarhet dypt i hjertet, den har
en munn som gaper og svelger uten å drikke.

Til denne verden hører også kvinnenes små lykker:
en katt i fanget, lave ord til barn
og alt som vokser, trådene i en vev
tre fingerspor på vinduene om aftenen,
det er for smått til å nevne men det er
kanskje det lave gresset i vårt liv,
den grønne bølgen som skyller om strandens sten
og bekken med den hvite panden,
tankeløs, full av musikk.

Unthinking—

Within every day there is a small heart
and an open hand.
Perhaps each day is a life in itself.
The morning has its law and so does the evening
and at night there is a crown of fire above our house
that no one can reach.

The summer brook's little white brow
is full of thoughts it can't hold onto
and belongs in another world, crystal pure
but more fleeting, always music.

The spruce cone falls like the stroke of a gong
and some nights are full of a bronzelike light.
The trout wanders in its river like a trail
of fertility deep in the heart, it has
a mouth that gapes and swallows without drinking.

To this world too belong women's small delights:
a cat in the lap, soft words to children
and everything that grows, the threads on a loom,
three finger-tracks on the windows in the evening—
they are too small to name but they are
perhaps the low grass in our life,
the green wave that washes around stones on the beach
and the brook with the white brow,
unthinking, full of music.

Avignon, Vaucluse

Under skyenes cumulus-tre en by på sletten
med mørke brystvern og tårnenes knudrede kuber.

Som et underlig hus i mørkningen. Guds bier
stillet ut under skyenes tre, mellem valmuene og vinen.

Summende av liv er den i aften, myldrende i alle vinkler
som en rasende bisverm når den ikke kan finne honningen.

Den har bannere i gull og sort, ridderrustninger med jernklør
og solens giftbrodd satt inn midt mellem øynene.

Men selv i de dypeste gater er det gullskjær over husene
som minner om voksplatene i tømte bikuber, sier du.

Om natten kom regnet. Da klokkene brummet midnatt
ble alt sløret til av et underlig røkflor, som silketøy.

Og dette, sier du vennlig, er biavlerens slør og hansker.
Nu tar han ut honningen og setter inn sukkervannet.

Avignon, Vaucluse

Under the clouds' cumulus-tree, a city on the plains
with dark breastwork and the towers' knobby hives.

Like a curious house in the dusk. God's bees
set out under the tree of clouds, between the poppies and the vines.

It's buzzing with life this evening, teeming in every corner
like a furious swarm of bees when they can't find the honey.

It has banners of gold and black, knight's armor with iron hands
and the sun's poisonous sting stuck right between its eyes.

But even in the deepest streets there is a golden sheen to
    the houses
that recalls the plates of wax in emptied beehives, you say.

At night the rain came. When the bells thrummed midnight
everything was veiled in a strange misty crepe, like a garment
    of silk.

And this, you say amiably, is the beekeeper's veil and gloves.
Now he's taking out the honey and putting in the sugar water.

fra HEADLINES

≈ ≈ ≈ ≈ ≈

1969

from HEADLINES

≈ ≈ ≈ ≈ ≈

1969

Ventetid

Noen står ute i solen og venter andre
venter ved bensinstasjoner kaféer
er gode å vente i du kan sitte
og tenke på hva som kan hende
om det ikke inntreffer
det du er redd for håper på
er likegyldig med iallfall
ventetid
i sykesengen på oboslisten eller
i billettkøen alderdoms-
hjemmet men mest
venter vi på det
som aldri hender eller
hender hver dag like-
gyldig gutt eller pike eller
på døden rikstelefonen
og postmannen men mest
på det som gjør glad
det lille
du holder gjemt i hånden
det lillelille
du holder skjult
forsiktig
i den ene hånden.

Waiting Time

Some stand out in the sun and wait others
wait at gas stations cafés
are good to wait in you can sit
and think about what can happen
if what you're afraid of hope for
are indifferent to doesn't
happen at any rate
waiting time
in the sickbed on the Oslo Housing list or
in the ticket-line the old-age
home but mostly
we wait for what
never happens or
happens every day un-
important boy or girl or
for death the long-distance call
and the mailman but mostly
for what gladdens
the little
you keep hidden in your hand
the little little
you hold hidden
carefully
in one hand.

Hyss— —

Hyss sier havet.
Hyss sier den lille bølgen ved stranden—hyss
ikke så voldsomme, ikke
så stolte ikke
så bemerkelsesverdige.
Hyss
sier bølgekammene som
flokker seg om forbergene
strandbrenningene. Hyss
sier de til menneskene
det er *vår* jord
vår evighet.

Hush— —

Hush says the ocean.
Hush says the little wave at the shore—hush
not so violent, not
so proud not
so eager for attention.
Hush
say the breakers that
pile up at the headlands,
the surf at the beaches. Hush
they say to us—
it's *our* world
our eternity.

Bonde-norge

Fjellene på frontruten, så sandelig
der dukker de opp igjen
bonde-norges grå støvler, veltet i haug.
—Selv er de under torven men støvlene
ligger her efter dem
gråe av støv, tungt regn og sorg.
Vindusviskerne vasker dem ikke bort.

Selv ute i havet ligger det hauger av steinstøvler
—tusener av dem—som fjell,
kaldvasket, skjeve og grå.
Hauger av døde
dager, hauger av år.
Vindusviskerne
vasker dem ikke bort.

Peasant Norway

With the mountains in the windshield, I swear
they turn up again:
peasant Norway's gray boots, piled in a heap.
—They themselves are under the sod but the boots
still lie here
gray with dust, heavy rain and sorrow.
The windshield wipers don't wash them away.

Even out in the sea there are heaps of stone boots
—thousands of them—like mountains,
washed in cold water, crooked and gray.
Heaps of dead
days, heaps of years.
The windshield wipers
won't wash them away.

Noen

Noen
stiger ut av vårt liv, noen
kommer inn i vårt liv
ubedt og setter seg ned,
noen
går likegyldige forbi, noen
skjenker deg en rose,
kjøper en ny bil,
noen
står deg meget nær, noen
har du alt glemt,
noen, noen
er deg selv,
noen
har du aldri sett, noen
spiser asparges, noen
er barn,
noen går opp på taket,
sitter ved et bord,
ligger i hengekøye, går med rød
paraply,
noen ser på deg,
noen har aldri lagt merke til deg, noen
vil holde deg i hånden, noen
døde i natt,
noen er andre, noen er deg, noen
er ikke,
noen er.

Some

Some
step out of our lives, some
come into our lives
unasked and sit down,
some
pass by indifferently, some
present you with a rose,
buy a new car,
some
are very close to you, some
you've already forgotten,
some, someone
is yourself,
some
you have never seen, some
are eating asparagus, some
are children,
someone is going up on the roof,
sitting at a table,
lying in a hammock, holding a red
umbrella,
some are looking at you,
some have never noticed you, some
want to hold your hand, some
died tonight,
some are others, some are you, some
are not,
some are.

Menneskepike—

Menneskepike jeg kan høre din tå
forsiktig når den beskrider mitt gulv
fremdeles
uten å forstyrres puster du
regelmessig du blir sulten
fire ganger om dagen og
drar meg i håret av ren velvilje også i deg
bor det en annen også på deg
venter sykesalene og døden men
du maler veggene blå og
hører andres ord med oppmerksomhet.

Din regelmessige pust om natten
når du hviler efter latter
beroliger meg. Drøm om fugler
drøm deg små barn som biter
deg i fingertuppene
ennu en gang. Pike det er mere
i verden, tidsepoker, galaksenes
islys og de magiske skyer av gasstøv
utenfor vår tanke forvandlet til gress
og til trær og til
dine bryster
er deler av en stjernes lys, vår
stjerne, liten men behagelig å puste i,
med litt for korte opphold pr. slektsledd
til å skape oss den dypere innsikt
—hver gang
må vi starte på nytt. Derfor
denne ustanselige uro.
Vi får ikke nok,
motivene
er for små kanskje billettprisen
for lav.

≈

Girlchild—

Girlchild I can hear your tiptoe
proceeding cautiously across my floor
still hear it
undisturbed you breathe
evenly, you get hungry
four times a day and
tug at my hair out of sheer sweetness in you too
there lives another for you too
the hospital wards and death are waiting but
you paint the walls blue and
listen attentively to people's words.

Your even breathing at night
when you're resting from laughter
brings me calm. Dream of birds
dream yourself little children who bite
your fingertips
yet again. Girl there is more
in the world, eons, the icy light
of galaxies and magical clouds of gas and dust
beyond our imagining transformed into grass
and trees and into
your breasts
are made from the light of a star, our
star, small but comfortable for breathing,
with visits per generation slightly too short
to grant us the deepest insight
—each time
we have to start over. Therefore
this endless unease.
We don't get enough,
the plot
is a bit thin maybe the price of admission
is too low.

≈

Sov nu,
snart springer lysene frem i en ny morgen
av livet ovenpå døden.
Bare en centimeter ned er det endeløst.
Mange går rundt med forhåpninger
om penger og nye løsninger
ventes å dukke opp,
men hos deg
som rolig er sovnet inn over billedbåndet
ordner skyene seg nu i rekker
som dine dagers hvite tallerkenhyller
og stiller seg rolig opp over et lydløst landskap
rød-munnet og stort av søvn.

Sleep now,
soon the light will leap out in a new morning
of life on top of death.
Just one centimeter down it's bottomless.
So many walk around with hopes
of money and new solutions
are expected to turn up,
but in you,
peacefully fallen asleep over your passing images
the clouds arrange themselves in rows now
like daytime's white rows of china
and line up quietly over a silent landscape,
red-lipped and puffy with sleep.

Vintertegn

Frosten knytter hendene og vil sprenge veibanene i stykker.
Aspenes løv er drept med formalinkapsler.
Is-breene sleper seg skritt for skritt over dal-toppene
tunge i baken og forpustet—en meter på tusen år.
Skyene er grimet av tretthet, varmer sine fingre
på en mørkerød sol. Fuglene
har tømt sine trær og reist bort i avmakt. Tungen
vender seg innover i din gane.
Tanken låser sin dør.

Signs of Winter

Frost clenches its fists and tries to shatter the roads.
The aspen leaves die with formaldehyde on their breath.
The glaciers drag themselves step by step across the heads
     of valleys,
bottom-heavy and winded—a meter every thousand years.
The clouds are streaked with fatigue, warm their fingers
on a dark-red sun. The birds
have left their trees empty and gone away defeated. Your tongue
curls back on your palate.
Thought locks its door.

Veis ende

Veiene er nu kommet til enden,
de kommer ikke lenger, de snur her,
borte på jordet der.
Det er ikke mulig å komme lenger hvis
De ikke vil til månen eller planetene. Stans nu
i tide og bli til hvepsebol eller ku-tråkk,
vulkanrør eller steinrammel i skogene
—det er det samme. Noe annet.

De kommer ikke lenger har jeg sagt
uten forvandling, motoren til hesteromper plutselig
girstangen til en grankvist
som De holder slapt i hånden
— — hva faen var dette?

End of the Road

This is where the roads end, you see
they don't go any further, they turn back here,
over at that field.
It's impossible to go further unless
you're heading for the moon or the planets. Stop while
there's time and become wasp's nest or cow path,
volcano's vent or rockslide in the forest
—it doesn't matter. Something else.

You can't go any further I'm telling you
without transformation: the motor into a horse's rump suddenly
the stick shift into a pine branch
that you hold loosely in your hand
— — what the hell is this?

Til Iris

Farvene bor hos deg
bare hos deg
grønt gult indigo og fiolett
bare hos deg—i øyet ditt
inne bak smilet der, utenfor er allting
natt avskyelig av elektroner
farveløst—helt blåst.
Bare hos deg—inne bak øyet der
er farvene til.
Tenk på det.

Hele regnbuen er hos deg
(bare regnværet hos meg)
farven på kjolen din, negle-
lakken, rosen, dåpsattesten
bare i øyet der
og ikke utenfor.
Tenk på det.

Det er øynene dine som kler verden på
—grønt, gult, indigo og fiolett
—bukser jakke sko og kam i håret.
Tenk på det.

To Iris

The colors live in you
only in you
green gold indigo and violet
only in you—in your eye
in there behind your smile; outside everything is
night abominable made of electrons
colorless—totally bare.
Only in you—in there behind your eye
do the colors exist.
Imagine that.

The whole rainbow is in you
(only rainfall in me)
the color of your dress, nail-
polish, rose, birth certificate
only in your eye
and not outside it.
Imagine that.

It is your eyes that clothe the world
—green, gold, indigo and violet
—pants jacket shoes and the combs in your hair.
Imagine that.

fra PASS FOR DØRENE —
DØRENE LUKKES

≈ ≈ ≈ ≈ ≈

1972

from WATCH THE DOORS —
THE DOORS ARE CLOSING

≈ ≈ ≈ ≈ ≈

1972

Grønn mann

Gå
sier den grønne mannen i trafikklyset
til alle bukseben bag'er barnevogner
brilleglass og brystholdere, få med deg
bena for nå haster det
med verden med vesten med østen med
varehuskjeder vinimport vekselfrister vel-
standsutvikling vannforurensning og voff-
voff. Få med deg bena, kom over for nå . . .

Stopp
sier den røde mannen
som er den samme som den grønne
mannen men i rødt, stille nå
og se hvor langsomt det går
med verden og vreden og vold-
somheten og vantrivselen
når de andre skal prøve seg. Stille
nå, helt stille, med solreiser og
sommerhusplaner. Hold kjeft nå men
bare i førti sek . . .

Gå
sier den grønne
gå bare gå
med deres verden voldtekt
valium og vacuumpakninger.
Gå
—dere har
i nøyaktig astronomisk tid
bare førti sekunder.

Green Man

Go
says the green man in the traffic light
to all the pant-legs shopping bags baby-buggies
bifocals and brassieres, get
a move on because now it's urgent
for the world for the west for the east for
wider markets wine-imports warranty dead-
lines wealth of nations water pollution and woof-
woof. Get a move on, come on! because now . . .

Stop
says the red man
who is the same as the green
man but in red, quiet now
and see how slowly change comes
to the world and the rage and the
frenzy and the resentment
when others are having a go. Quiet
now, completely quiet about sunny vacations and
summer-cottage plans. Shut up now but
only for forty sec . . .

Go
says the green
go just go
with your world rape
valium and vacuum-packing.
Go
—you have
in precise astronomical time
only forty seconds.

Kniver kniver

Kniver kniver overalt de skjærer
verden opp med kniver
uten nåde og vi må gå med på det
for de skal se alt på innsiden
hva det er gjort av
alle ting din sjel og fuglesangen
skal snittes opp og legges frem for dommerne
dagdrømmer parringslyst og frykt for døden
men noe er gått galt for dem
de får det ikke sammen igjen vil ikke gro
blir liggende som slaktet kjøtt vrakstykker
gule ben
men knivene fortsetter å skjære
noe tas bort og tas bort hver dag
og avfallsdyngene blir stadig større
—jeg er redd. Snart ringer de hit
fra renholdsverket.

Knives Knives

Knives knives everywhere they're cutting
the world up with knives
mercilessly and we have to go along with it
for they *must* see the inside of everything
what it's made of
all things your soul and the birdsong
must be sliced up and laid out for the judges
daydreams mating-drive and fear of death
but something's gone wrong
they can't get it back together it will not heal
just lies there like butchered meat waste and scraps
yellowed bones
but the knives continue to cut
something's carved away and carved away each day
and the refuse piles keep getting bigger
—I'm afraid. Soon we'll be getting a call
from the sanitation department.

Angelus

Mirakler som hender omigjen
er ikke lenger mirakler
blir snart likegyldigheter som ansikter i en buss
eller den frosne elven av stjernelys
som strømmer langsomt over huset ditt om natten
også når du er død og opptatt av andre ting.
Hva vet du om dette. Det gamle
du ser deroppe statisk og fosforskimrende
er kanskje verdens sperma, Guds sæd, som flommer
og jorden den du står på er cellen
den ene den benådede
med fosterhinnen og med fødselsskriket.
«—Se han har sett sin tjenerinnes ringhet.
Fra nå skal alle slekter prise mig salig.»

Men vi skal dø snart og det gjelder å få med seg alt
bil kone og gressklipper og ikke tulle seg bort
med tanker som gjør deg rar. Alle har sitt.
Men av og til kan vi jo lure på
hva som egentlig foregår her.
For hva skal vi tro på da. Gamle historier
eller nye historier. Tusenårsriker eller Hva
sier stjernene.

Best ikke å hefte seg. For noe kan hende snart.
Og det gjelder å få med seg alt
som tyven sier
når huset tilfeldigvis står tomt
og det bare er en eldgammel sol
og en blindfødt måne som holder vakt.

Angelus

Miracles that happen over again
are no longer miracles,
soon become inconsequential like faces on a bus
or the frozen river of starlight
that flows slowly over your house at night
and will go on when you are dead and concerned with other things.
What can you know about all this. The old light
you see up there, unchanging and phosphorescent,
is perhaps the world's sperm, God's seed flowing
and the earth you are standing on is the cell
the one, the favored one
with the birth sac, the cry of birth.
"—Behold he hath regarded the low estate of his handmaiden;
from henceforth all generations shall call me blessed."

But we will die soon and the point is to get hold of everything
car wife and lawn mower and not get lost
in thoughts that make you odd. We all have our problems.
But once in a while we can certainly wonder
what is really going on here.
For, what shall we believe in anyway. Old stories
or new stories. The Millennium or
Your Horoscope.

Best not to take notice. For soon something may happen.
And the point is to get hold of everything
as the thief says
when by chance there is no one in the house
and only an ancient sun
and a moon blind from birth
are standing watch.

Briefing

Gud sa: De små.
La dem komme til meg.
Pst! Alle små. Over her. Still i kø
små hender silkesokker tanker
lys og luft små ord og gjerninger
små hus små land små dyr og blomster
revebjelle og linnea. De store
lar vi seile. Alle små
velkommen vær. Ikke så redde da.
Kom så.
Kom så. Og ta kanarifuglen med
for nå må vi tenke litt
på det som skjer. Vi må
bli sterkere på jorden støere
på bena ellers tar de oss
og putter oss i sekken
alle sammen—efter tur
hver silkesokk hver skygge lys og luft
alt som gjør jorden grønn
og himlen blå
små hus små land små brev
og små bokstaver bier
og maur og metemark
blås ikke bort men bli
hvor dere står.
Pass godt
på hodene.
Slipp ikke taket. Husk på
at jorden snurrer
rundt og rundt
og rundt og rundt
og at alt som er
kommer igjen
—også jeg. Sa Gud.

Briefing

God said: The small ones.
Let them come unto me.
Psst! All small ones. Over here. Line up
small hands silk socks thoughts
light and air small words and deeds
small houses small countries small animals and flowers
foxglove and honeysuckle. We'll leave
the big ones to their fate. All small ones
feel welcome. Not so afraid, then.
Come on, now.
Come on. And bring the canary along,
because now we have to think a bit
about what's happening. We must
be stronger on the earth steadier
on our feet or they'll take us
and put us all in the sack
— one after the other
each silk sock each shadow light and air
everything that makes the earth green
and the sky blue
small houses small countries small messages
and small letters bees
and ants and earthworms
don't blow away —
stay put.
Watch out
for your heads.
Don't lose your grip. Remember
that the earth spins
round and round
and round and round
and that everything that is
comes again
— me too. Said God.

Epilog

Til en radering: «Aurora», av Anne-Lise Knoff

Sol-nære, sol-fjerne,
førerløst i rommet går jorden
tungtlastet med barn og fugler,
skog-snar, sky-flekker og glassklare vinder
uten lyd og bak avstander
ennu skjønnere enn nattens
tåkeslør over hav-tummel. Barbados'
kyster eller Hebridenes.

Der de alltid motstridende
tiders meninger, protesttog, halvoppfylte
og aldri eller noenlunde bønnhørte
løper ut i sanden, våre håp
reddes fra flamme-ovnene og
knuses igjen i sutrende dagsbehov.
Til de reiser seg sky-flammende
mot Andromeda og Arcturus
og morgenen samler sine roser
kanskje bak døden, marmorhvit.
—For noen tror på håpet
stikk imot all forstand,
livet i dødens rom, dets
trossige stjerne.

Epilogue

For an etching: "Aurora," by Anne-Lise Knoff

Sun-approaching, sun-departing,
pilotless in space the world goes
heavily laden with children and birds,
forest thickets, cloud patches and winds clear as glass
soundless and beyond expanses
even more beautiful than the night's
veil of mist over sea-swell. The coasts of
Barbados or the Hebrides.

Where the opinions of the always
contentious times, the protest marches, half-successes
and the never or partly granted prayers
come to nothing, where our hopes
are saved from the flaming ovens and
ground down again in whining daily needs.
Until they rise up sky-blazing
toward Andromeda and Arcturus
and the morning gathers its roses
perhaps beyond death, marble-white.
—For some believe in hope
against all reason,
in life amid death's space, in its
obstinate star.

fra PUSTEØVELSE

≈ ≈ ≈ ≈ ≈

1975

from BREATHING EXERCISE

≋ ≋ ≋ ≋ ≋

1975

Skylab

Så langt er vi kommet, tenkte astronauten
da han svømte rundt i sin kabine på tredje uken
og av vanvare var kommet til å sparke en gud i øyet
—så langt
at det ikke lenger er forskjell på oppe eller nede,
syd eller nord, lett eller tungt.
Og hvordan kan vi da kjenne rettferdigheten.

Så langt.
Og vektløse, i et lukket rom
jager vi rundt efter soloppgangene i stor fart
og lengter oss syke efter et grønt strå
eller å få gripe fatt i noe som gjør motstand. Løfte en sten.

En natt så han at Jorden lignet et åpent øye
som så på ham alvorsfullt som et barns
når det er våknet midt på natten.

Skylab

We've come so far, thought the astronaut
as he swam around the capsule in his third week
and by accident kicked a god in the eye
—so far
that there's no difference anymore between up and down,
north and south, heavy and light.
And how, then, can we know righteousness.

So far.
And weightless, in a sealed room
we chase the sunrises at high speed
and sicken with longing for a green stalk
or the heft of something in our hands. Lifting a stone.

One night he saw that the Earth was like an open eye
that looked at him as gravely as the eye of a child
awakened in the middle of the night.

Hus av glass

De ynker seg litt de gamle husene når de faller.
Knark sier det når ytterveggen går.
Blupp sier det når kjøkkenvasken ramler ned i kjelleren
og krisj krasj sier det når stuegulvet sprekker.

Men så slipper regndråpene til der putesvetten var
og sengeknirket var og hvor alle ordene ble sagt,
nytt kaldt regn som vasker bort alle riftene i luften,
nervespenningen og de onde ordene og hjertedunket
som sitter fast i luften som en hinne, et hus av glass.

Det er så greit med gamle hus,
de er ikke skrevet ned noe sted,
kan bare brettes sammen som en avis,
som et vift i luften, kyss som begge har glemt,
sorgene fra i går.

A Glass House

The old houses groan a little when they fall.
"Knark" they say when the outer wall goes.
"Bloop" says the kitchen sink when it collapses into the basement
and "Crish crash" says the living-room floor when it splits.

But then the raindrops get a chance where sweat lay on the pillow
and the bed creaked and where all the words were said,
cold new rain that washes away all the rifts in the air,
the nervous tension and the cruel words and the heartbeats
that are stuck in the air like a membrane, a glass house.

How convenient old houses are,
they're not written down anywhere,
can just be folded up like a newspaper,
like a waft of air, kisses that both people have forgotten,
yesterday's sorrows.

Antenneskog

Oppe på byenes tak er det store sletter.
Dit krøp stillheten opp da det ikke var plass til den på gatene.
Nå kommer skogen efter.
Den må være der hvor stillheten holder til.
Tre følger på tre i underlige lunder.
Den får det ikke riktig til for bunnen er for hard.
Det blir en glissen skog, en gren mot øst,
og en mot vest. Til det ligner på kors. En skog
av kors. Og vinden spør
—Hvem hviler her
i disse dype graver?

Antenna-forest

Up on the city's roofs there are large fields.
That's where silence crept up to
when there was no room for it on the streets.
Now the forest comes in its turn.
It needs to be where silence lives.
Tree upon tree in strange groves.
They don't do very well, because the floor is too hard.
So they make a sparse forest, one branch toward the east,
and one toward the west. Until it looks like crosses. A forest
of crosses. And the wind asks
—Who's resting here
in these deep graves?

Avaldsnes

Gamle stentårn når natten faller på
kan ligne stubbene efter digre trær.
Vi kom til Avaldsnes en aften og fikk se
en gammel kirke mørkne på sin haug,
innvevd i hvite tåkeflor, en gråstensklump
som lignet mest på roten til et tre,
en kjempe-eik, en ask som engang har ruvet her
med fuglesang og med grenene spredt ut
over et hardbygd, underlig land.
Kanskje en Yggdrasil, kanskje et stridere tre,
nedblåst i tidenes vind
da grenene ble for tunge
og stormen kanskje for svær,
men hvor fløy fuglene hen,
hvor ble sangene av,
si meg det?

Avaldsnes

Old stone towers at nightfall
can resemble the stumps of giant trees.
We came to Avaldsnes one evening and saw
an old church grow dark on its hill,
woven into a white veil of mist: a granite clump
that looked like the root of a tree,
a mighty oak or ash that once loomed here
with birdsong and with branches spread out
above a rugged, mysterious land.
Perhaps an Yggdrasil, perhaps a tougher tree,
blown down in the wind of the ages
when its branches got too heavy
and the storm perhaps too severe;
but where did the birds fly off to,
what became of their songs,
can you tell me that?

Små byer i Auvergne

De små byene i Auvergne
oppe på hvert sitt fjell og under hver sin sky
ligger stille og samler støv
og samler tid.
De samler år som biene samler honning
og gjemmer dem bort på sine loft og i kjølige hvelv.
De har tårn som ligner knyttede never
og murer av glemt sol
de små byene i Auvergne,
brune som kobberstikk
mørkner de inn i natten og lysner mot neste dag.
De har små torv som blusser opp som roser
og smale gater som kommer ut av mørket og vil holde deg i hånden
og følge deg frem til kirken St. Hippolyte
hvor Josef og Maria står tause på sine sokler
og stirrer med stive øyne ut over et stengrått land,
om noe hjelper.

De små byene i Auvergne
(og i Dordogne og Tarn og Puy-de-Dôme)
hvor det lukter myrjord og sau og vissent løv
og elvene gjemmer seg bort i trange daler
og hvor solen oser av vin og søler den ut på skyene
—dit kommer stjernene om natten og drysser sine saltkorn,
de bitre, over berg og bakker
og de små byene i Auvergne—at de skal holde seg karske
og stille
ennå en tid.

Old Cities in Auvergne

The old cities of Auvergne
each one up on its own mountain and under its own cloud
lie still and gather dust
and gather time.
They collect years as the bees collect honey
and hide them away in their attics and in cool vaults.
They have towers that look like clenched fists
and walls of forgotten sun,
the old cities of Auvergne;
brown as copperplate prints
they darken into the night and brighten toward the next day.
They have small markets that blaze up like roses
and narrow streets that emerge from the dark and want to hold
    your hand
and lead you to the Church of St. Hippolyte
where Joseph and Mary stand silent on their pedestals
and stare out across a stone-gray land with stiff eyes
to see if anything will help.

The old cities of Auvergne
(and of Dordogne and Tarn and Puy-de-Dôme)
where it smells of bog and sheep and withered leaves
and the rivers hide themselves away in narrow valleys
and where the sun is drenched in wine and spills it onto the clouds
—the stars come there at night and sprinkle their bitter grains
    of salt
over mountains and hillsides
and the old cities of Auvergne—so they will stay hardy
and still
yet another while.

Garnpinner, nål og tråd

Gamle kniplinger har en duft av skyldfrihet,
ligner for tidlige snefall
eller rimfrosten over døde trær.

Millefleur-gobelinene tar deg med inn i en have
hvor det alt er blitt høst. De er vevet av døde roser
og vissent gress.

Det går en tråd, tynn, gjennom alle tider
som prøver å binde tingene sammen,
fange en drøm, men det blir borte.

Tynne nåler, løpende fingre, bøyde nakker.
Ventetider. Sønnene i krigen. Alt de hadde tenkt seg
men som aldri ble av.

Det står et blekrødt merke på ditt kinn en morgen.
Fra puten. En bokstav
som noen sydde der med falmet garn.

Needles, Thread and Yarn

Old lacework has an air of innocence,
like premature snowfall
or hoarfrost on dead trees.

The millefleur Gobelins take you along to a garden
where autumn has already arrived. They are woven of dead roses
and withered grass.

Through all ages there runs a thread
that tries to tie things together,
capture a dream, but it gets away.

Thin needles, flying fingers, bent necks.
Times of waiting. Sons in the war. Everything they'd imagined
that never came about.

One morning there's a pale red mark on your cheek.
From the pillow. A single letter
that someone sewed there with faded yarn.

Hallingskeid

Ut og inn av tunnellene,
tilslutt en som er lang nok
til at du kan speile ansiktet ditt i fjellveggen
midt mellom såpeannonsene og banksparingen
og tenke over ditt liv og dine forsømmelser,
til lyset kommer igjen som en smerte mot øynene
og forteller at du er inne i en annen dal
enn hva du trodde først og bak et annet fjell,
helt anderledes enn det du hadde tenkt,
eftersom alt med økende hast forvandles
til det motsatte av hva vi venter på,
til baksider, ur og stenrøys, ødsligheter
av verdensdimensjoner, månelandskaper
er det vi ser bre seg ut ved Reinunga og Såta,
isglitrende breer som siler ned i en dal, dypt,
svimlende glaner vi ned gjennom skyene, plutselig et hus,
dukkesmått, for mennesker, veier som sytråd,
et utsnitt av levende bindevev mens hjulene her,
tamtaratam-tamtaratam, smatrer som mitraljøseild
og vognen sover, hodene nikker i takt
bak avisoverskrifter og bilder av fjerne katastrofer
og lyset slukkes og kommer igjen
som solgitre og skyggehuller, vi er flyttet
over i ennu en dal, tåkelagt
og med glimt av is
som en ny slags jord, en ny slags frykt,
en ny slags undring og fortapelse,
—litt sent nå, kan du si, å våkne opp
til nye avsindige morgener og kjøpe nye billetter
og stige av på en stasjon hvor ingenting er kjent
og alle snur seg efter deg med trette øyne
—er han en av våre eller skal vi hate ham
her i vår nye verden av kraftmaster og stenblokker
og hvor det mørkner og lysner vekselvis i skift
som om de ennu ikke har bestemt seg, skjønt nu haster det
for vi nærmer oss vannskillet, minutt for minutt
stiger vi stadig oppover mellom ustanselige fjell,

Hallingskeid

In and out of the tunnels,
finally one that is long enough
so you can see your face mirrored in the wall of rock
right between the soap ads and the savings plans
and can think over your life and your derelictions,
until the light returns like a pain to your eyes
and tells you that you are in a different valley
than you thought at first and behind a different mountain,
completely unlike what you had thought,
since everything is transformed at increasing speed
into the opposite of what we expect,
into back ends, scree and stone-piles,
wastelands on a planetary scale, moonscapes
are what we watch spreading out near Reinunga and Såta,
ice-sparkling glaciers that pour deep into a valley;
dizzily we gaze down through the clouds, suddenly a house,
as small as for dolls, but for people, roads like thread,
a section of living tissue while here the wheels,
tomtaratom-tomtaratom, rattle like machine-gun fire
and the railway car sleeps, the heads nod in rhythm
behind newspaper headlines and pictures of distant catastrophes
and the light is shut off and comes back
in sun-grilles and shadow-holes, we have moved
over into yet another valley, obscured by mist
and glinting with ice
like a new kind of earth, a new kind of fear,
a new kind of awe and doom
—a little late now, you may say, to wake up
to new crazy mornings and buy new tickets
and get off at a station where nothing is familiar
and everyone follows you with weary eyes
—is he one of ours or shall we hate him
here in our new world of power lines and stone blocks
where it gets dark and light alternately in shifts
as if they still haven't decided, though now it's urgent
for we're coming to the divide, minute by minute
we climb steadily upward between unending mountains,

ut og inn gjennom mørket til bremsene skriker
inne i en ny natt, vi ser
en lykt som svinger, lys i et nakent vindu,
et pift under sneoverbygget. Vi står i mørket.
Lydløst. Hva venter vi på.
Og hvor lenge.

in and out through the darkness until the brakes screech
inside a new night, we see
a lantern swinging, light in a bare window, hear
a whistle under the snow shelter. We wait in the darkness.
Silently. What are we waiting for.
And for how long.

Blinde ord

—er ord som elskere sier med sin hud
inne i nattens rom hvor ingen tanker har form.

—er ord som den døende former i sin strupe
og aldri får sagt før lysene er brent ned.

—er ord som fosteret sier når det drømmer
om lyder det ikke kan høre og farver det ikke vet.

—er ord som vinden sier til treet og sorgene
til vårt hjerte.

—ord som var her før ordene ble til,
som jorden er gjort av
og som stjernene sender ut som lys
i tidløse åndedrag.

Blind Words

—are words that lovers say with their skin
inside night's space, where thoughts are without form.

—are words the dying person forms in his throat
and never gets said before the candles have burned down.

—are words the fetus says when it dreams
about sounds it cannot hear and colors it doesn't know.

—are words the wind says to the tree and sorrows
say to our heart.

—words that were here before words were created,
words that the earth is made of
and that the stars exhale as light
in their timeless breathing.

Sand

Det finnes et nøyaktig tall for alle sandkorn på jorden
såvelsom for stjerneverdnene over våre hoder,
(Det skal være like mange) hvis vi bare hadde kjent det,
men av større betydning er det å vite at sandkornene
blir stadig flere og ørknene større. Et stenk
av fiolett har blandet seg i solnedgangenes rosa.

Sand er hvit som melk og myk
som et strøk av fioliner.
Sand kysser foten din
og risler over håndflatene som rent vann.
Ved Bir el Daharrem er berg og daler gjort av bronce.
Ved Theben og Asmara ligger døde byer under sanden.

Sand er knuste fjell og asken efter alt som har vært.
Sandfluktene går over hete land som striper av ild.
Sand dekker klodene. Månestrålene er gjenskinn i sand.
Sand er det siste på jorden.
Sovende tid.

Sand

There is a precise total for all the grains of sand on earth,
as well as for the starry worlds above our heads
(supposedly the same for each), if only we knew it,
but it's more important to know that the grains of sand
grow constantly in number and the deserts are getting bigger.
    A touch
of violet has mixed itself into the pink of sunset.

Sand is white as milk and soft
as a bowing of violins.
Sand kisses your foot
and trickles over your palms like clean water.
At Bir el Daharrem hills and valleys are made of bronze.
At Thebes and Asmara dead cities lie under the sand.

Sand is crushed mountains and the ashes of everything that has
    existed.
The sand dunes cross hot countries like stripes of fire.
Sand covers the planets. Moonbeams are reflections in sand.
Sand is the last thing on earth.
Time sleeping.

Uten en lyd

Lydløsheten inne i alt som hender.
Det stummes tyngde. Lyset
som faller på et ansikt
som forandringer, ikke som fred.

Noen står der og vet ikke at de er til.
Lyder faller til jorden. Regn
splintres som glass.

Det umåtelige har ingen stemme.
Det som betyr noe. Ikke nattemørket.
Ikke sollyset. Ikke døden.

Without a Sound

The silence within everything that happens.
The weight of the unspoken. The light
that falls on a face
like changes, not like peace.

Some people stand there and don't know they exist.
Sounds fall to the earth. Rain
shatters like glass.

What is intense has no voice.
Whatever means something. Not the dark of night.
Not the sunlight. Not death.

I bringebærtiden

I bringebærtiden
kommer vepsene inn i huset,
og finner ikke ut igjen, dag efter dag
dasker de mot rutene, summe-summe-summ
til vi kan feie dem ut på søplebrettet.

Også for deg og meg
er det stengsler vi ikke kan forstå.
Vi kaster oss gang efter gang mot noe vi ikke kan se
til de feier oss ut en dag på søplebrettet.
Om ikke noen på jorderik eller i skyene
tilfeldigvis
skulle sette opp et vindu så vi kommer igjennom.

In Raspberry Season

In raspberry season
the wasps come into the house
and can't find their way out again; day after day
they dash against the windowpanes, sooma-sooma-soom
until we can sweep them out on the dustpan.

For you and me too
there are barriers we can't understand.
Time after time we throw ourselves against something we
    cannot see
until they sweep us out one day on the dustpan.
Unless, by chance,
someone on this earth or in the clouds
raises a window so we get through.

Ovenfra, nedenfra og fra siden

Fuglesløret om jorden kan ikke sees fra satellittene
men er der allikevel som et fjærlett dirr av vingeslag,
små hamrende hjerter og lynskarpe øyenpar
fotograferer vår hverdag som spionsondene, men de sladrer ikke.
Nattergalen gjemmer på en sorg.

Sett fra siden ser du tingene bedre. Alt får profil.
Smør og ost. De hule kinnene. De innsunkne øynene.
Skyene er deroppe som hierarkier av dikt og drøm.
Hvorfor skjelver du på hånden?

Sett underfra er allting stort. Som hos gudene.
Metemarken tror det tordner når du setter tåen ned.
Fra den dødes synspunkt er det du som er i himlen.

From Above, from Below and from the Side

The veil of birds around the earth can not be seen from the
    satellites
but is there just the same, as a feather-light tremor of beating
    wings;
small hammering hearts and lightning-sharp double lenses
photograph our days like the orbiting spies, but they don't tell.
The nightingale cherishes a sorrow.

From the side you see things better. Everything gets clearer.
Butter and cheese. The hollow cheeks. The sunken eyes.
The clouds above are like hierarchies of song and dream.
Why is your hand trembling?

Seen from underneath everything is large. As among the gods.
The earthworm thinks it's thundering when you put your toe
    down.
From the dead's point of view, it's you who are in heaven.

Stenhistorien

—er sent fortalt
for det er så mye av den
og så tungt

som Babels murer
og ingen som kan si oss navn
på dem som tok fjellene ned
og satte dem opp igjen som festninger,
fangehull og tårn.

Verden er stiv av herrer
og tung av keiserslott.
Murene ligger igjen efter dem som skorper,
stenbruddene som arr.

For dødsfrykten er overalt
og herreveldene er overalt
og menneskehjertene holder aldri opp å slå
—hammer mot sten, hammer mot sten
så lenge tiden er til.

The History of Stone

—is late in being told
because there is so much of it
and it's so heavy

like Babel's walls
and there is no one who can tell us the names
of those who took down the mountains
and put them up again as fortresses,
dungeons and towers.

The world is stiff with masters
and heavy with the palaces of czars.
Their walls are left behind like scabs,
the quarries like scars.

For the fear of death is everywhere
and the dominions of masters are everywhere
and human hearts never stop beating
—hammer on stone, hammer on stone
as long as time goes on.

Vi som bor ved jernbanen

Dagene går. Og eftersom alt får litt mindre glans
fordi det gjentar seg og gjentar seg som avisoppslagene
og ruteboken, er det mye som kan sjaltes ut som mindre
maktpåliggende såsom brevandringer i tørrsne
eller innkjøp av farvefjernsyn.
Men ikke togene. Ikke for meg.
Jeg mener tog som nabo. Hengende over havegjerdet.
Og tog langt inni tinningene. Som jordskjelv.

Jeg er bofast ved en bane. (Utsikt til en sjø)
Har skinnene utenfor veggen. (Solnedgangene er vakre her)
Og som sagt tog.

Nok av dem.
Under vinduet nattetid 2,55, 3,20 og 3,55
som billedserier, filmstriper, fragmenter
av andres liv, dertil nattoget 5,15
med sne på takene, frisk fra Dovrefjell.

Alt går over. Og fort.
Blåser det en vind mot øst, stormer det straks
mot vest. Og omvendt for at verden alltid
skal befinne seg i balanse
og ikke styrte sammen over malmtoget
som løfter deg opp av dynene 3,35
og ber deg om å Huske-huske-huske-huske
at du lever på en vulkan.

Ens posisjon blir derfor lett: betrakterens.
Alt går over. Sitte og se.
Strømninger i tiden. Ufred og godt vær.
Kvinneår, oljeproblemer og flom
i Gudbrandsdalslågen.

≈

We Who Live near the Railway

The days go by. And since everything loses a little luster
because it repeats itself and repeats itself like the newspaper
    headlines
and the timetables, there's a lot that can be dropped as less
pressing, for example hikes on glaciers in powder snow
or buying a color television.
But not the trains. Not for me.
I mean trains as neighbors. Leaning over the backyard fence.
And trains deep in my temples. Like earthquakes.

I make my home near a railroad. (View of a lake)
Have the rails outside my wall. (Sunsets are pretty here)
And as I said, trains.

No shortage of them.
Under the window at 2:55, 3:20 and 3:55 A.M.
like the comics, strips of film, fragments
of other people's lives, and then the night train at 5:15
with snow on the car-roofs, fresh from the Dovre Mountains.

Everything passes. And fast.
If a wind blows toward the east, there's soon a storm
in the west. And vice versa, so the world
will always be in balance
and won't cave in on top of the ore train
that raises you from the eiderdowns at 3:35
to insist-insist-insist-insist
that you're living on a volcano.

So one's position easily becomes the observer's.
Everything passes. Sit and watch.
Currents in time. Unrest and good weather.
Women's Year, oil problems, and another flood
in Gudbrandsdalen.

≈

Fire kilometer hver natt, bare av gods,
for ikke å snakke om dagens
tredobbelte ekspresser. Jeg kan se
et bånd av ansikter blekne bak avisene
som lynblinkene i august. Tordenen kommer efterpå.
Alt blir en vane. Hold munn og lukk vinduene.
Og så kommer stillheten.

Det varte ikke så lenge som jeg trodde.
Årene går, pendelen svinger, den er av jern
og tung: Syd-nord, tikk-takk, nord-syd. Sitte og se
at alt går over. Til tiden er inne
for nattoget, hvis det holder ruten.
Jeg hører det alt,
først som et stille piano-pianissimo, tam-tarratam.
Derefter sterkere, som et drønn. Her har vi det
nattsvart og med tause vinduer, vogn efter vogn,
åtte boggier i natt og snefaner mellom koblingene
friske fra Fokkstumyrene og Hjerkinnhø.

Four kilometers every night, just of freight,
not to mention the day's
extra-long expresses. I can see
a band of faces behind their newspapers, flashing by
as pale as lightning in August. The thunder comes afterwards.
Everything becomes a habit. Keep quiet, close the windows.
And then comes the silence.

It didn't last as long as I thought.
The years go by, the pendulum swings, it is iron
and heavy: south-north, tick-tock, north-south. Sit and watch
how everything passes. Until it's time
for the night train, if it's on schedule.
I hear it already,
at first as a quiet piano-pianissimo, tom-tarratom.
And then much stronger, like a booming. Here it is,
night-black and with silent windows, car after car,
eight sleepers tonight and banners of snow between the couplers
fresh from the Fokkstu Bogs and the Hjerkinn Dome.

fra TENK PÅ NOE ANNET

≈ ≈ ≈ ≈ ≈

1979

from THINK ABOUT SOMETHING ELSE

≈ ≈ ≈ ≈ ≈

1979

Fasten your seat belts—

Å sitte fastklemt, med knærne under haken,
høyt over tordenværene og ripsbuskene,
slik ble vår skjebne når vi vil til de fjerne kyster.
Et lite glimt av Irland, moseskimlet
som i et velbrukt atlas, lynsnart
trekker de ullteppet over det igjen,
så vi skal skånes for å se det hele.
Og under det store teppet, grått efter mye vask
ligger også havet,
vannstjernen Jordens rynkede hud
som heller ikke liker for mange blikk.

Og så
kom natten,
med Jupiter, Andromeda og Sirius.
Og den som ved et tilfelle fikk vindusplassen
kan se ut på mørket, se galaxer, tåkefjerne
melkeveisystemer, verdensrommets urfjærer
som får hjertene til å tikke og gå,
tikk-takk, tikk-takk inne i alt av liv,
alt som beveger seg. På alle kloder.
Mennesker, elefanter, selv i sølvrevens trange bur
tikker det og går, hamrer det og går,
i redsel eller trygghet, elskov eller hat.
Også her, hos de 139 levende liv
15 000 fot over Atlanteren og bare 60
sjømil øst av Labrador
inne i et svevende rom som ligner en teatersalong

hvor publikum er sovnet under forestillingen,
til en liten sitring i skroget
får hjertene til å banke fortere igjen,
tikk-tikk-takk, men bare fremover, fremover
i et liv som ingen av oss vet slutten på,
eftersom hvert sekund du lever

Fasten Your Seat Belts —

To sit squeezed tight, with your knees up to your chin,
high above the thunderstorms and the currant bushes,
such is our fate when we set out for distant shores.
A glimpse of moss-like Ireland, mottled
as in a well-worn atlas, and quick as lightning
they pull the wool blanket over it again,
so we'll be spared the trouble of seeing all of it.
And under the vast blanket, gray after many washings,
lies the sea as well,
Earth-the-water-star's wrinkled skin,
which also avoids our stares.

And then
comes the night,
with Jupiter, Andromeda and Sirius.
And whoever by chance has the window seat
can look out at the dark, see galaxies, distant cloudy
milky ways, outer space's mainsprings
that make each heart tick and go,
tick-tock, tick-tock within everything living,
everything that moves. On all planets.
People, elephants, even in the silver fox's narrow cage
it ticks and goes, it pounds and goes,
in terror or safety, love or hate.
Here too, in the 139 living beings
15,000 feet above the Atlantic and only 60
nautical miles east of Labrador
inside a floating room that's like a theater

where the audience has dozed off during the performance,
until a slight vibration in the fuselage
sets the hearts beating faster again,
tick-tick-tock, but only forward, forward
in a life none of us knows the conclusion of,
since each second you live

er som spissen på en pil—din egen tid,
der du alt er blitt eldre efter første linje i diktet.
Så du må gjerne bla om. Men reis deg ikke og gå,
for vi er fremme snart
i den nye tiden, der snart alt er gjort av glass
og gjennomsiktig, for vi har fått nye øyne
og hårde. Du ser nesten alt som hender på Jorden.
Og gleden din blir langsomt dempet ned.

No smoking allowed.
Please fasten your seat belts.
Og så ned på jorden, til regnværet,
rulletrappene og drosjekøene.
Det er livet ditt
jeg skriver om.

is like the point of an arrow—your own time—
where you've already gotten older after the first line in the poem.
So by all means turn the page. But don't get up and leave,
because we'll be arriving soon
in the new era, where everything will soon be made of glass,
transparent, for we've acquired new eyes,
hard ones. You see almost everything that happens on Earth.
And your delight gets slowly subdued.

No smoking allowed.
Please fasten your seat belts.
And then the landing, down to the rain,
the escalators and the waiting-lines for taxis.
It is your life
I'm writing about.

Bildene

—har det lettvint nå.
Får gå rett inn i stua,
sofaen og den beste stolen.
Ordene
har fått lengre vei å gå,
kanskje må de hvile litt også,
kjemme håret eller tørke av skoene,
(det er litt sølete ofte)
så får de komme inn i stua, de også,
men ikke i sofaen.

The Images

—have it easy now.
Make themselves at home,
get the sofa and the best chair.
The words
have to take the long way around,
maybe they have to rest a while too,
comb their hair or clean off their shoes
(often the road's a bit muddy);
then they can come in too,
but they don't get the sofa.

Mediadiktet

Alt dette vi skal stappe inn i øynene våre nå.
Alle farvenes lyn og tordenvær, angstrop og skrik.
Trykksvertestrømmenes evige Niagara. Hver dag—hver dag.
Nilfloder av halvtenkte tanker. Følg med. Gi plass.
Press det sammen for det kommer mer. Hiv ut det gamle.
Ut med det. Det nye er viktigere. Hold takt
med tiden. Og den er NÅ.

Stapp det inn i øynene. Dytt på her. Inn med det.
Klem det sammen til forte slagord. Ingen plass mer
til lange forklaringer—eftertanker—. HIV DET UT.
Du har fått enda et øye nå, vet du,
så nå ser du hele verden—eller nesten.
(Det blir iallfall pene farver på det—kanskje ikke helt,
men bortimot.)

Å se det meste, vite nesten alt
kunne bare Vårherre (i sin tid).
Men var han glad for det? Det sa de ikke noe om.
For vi som lever nå blir aldri riktig glade mer.
Ikke som ungene, eller som liljene på marken, lerkesangen.
For det vi har sett og hørt går aldri bort igjen.
Torden og lyn. Vi fullstappes dag efter dag
som fra foringsmaskiner for broilerhjerner, tettpakket
i våre bur. — Det er bare å gape, så kommer det.
Og ingen har lov å unnslå seg. Du har å sitte der.

———

Idag er det blåsevær ute. Hele Mjøsa er hvit.
Sitte og se her på sneen og vinden
som skriver på den med usynlig blekk.
Puste en liten stund. Men ikke for lenge. Glad
får du lov til å bli. Men bare for små, små ting.
Og røm ikke tilskogs. Vi finner deg.

≈

The Media Poem

All this we're supposed to stuff into our eyes now.
All the colors' lightning and thunder, cries of anguish and screams.
An endless Niagara of printer's ink. Every day — every day.
Flooding Niles of half-formed thoughts. Keep up. Make room.
Cram it in, there's more on the way. Throw out what's old.
Out with it. What's new is more important. Keep pace
with the times. And that means NOW.

Stuff it into your eyes. Shove it in here. In with it.
Squeeze it into sound bites. No more room
for long explanations — reflections —. THROW THAT OUT.
You've gotten a third eye now, you know,
so now you see the whole world — or almost.
(It's got pretty colors, at any rate — maybe not perfect,
but close.)

To see and know almost everything —
only Our Lord could do that (in his day).
But did it make him happy? They didn't comment on that.
For we who live now are never really happy anymore.
Not like children, or the singing lark, the lilies of the field.
For what we've seen and heard never goes away again.
Thunder and lightning. We're stuffed full day after day
as if by feeding-machines for brains like chickens, packed tight
in our coops. — Just open wide and it comes.
And no one is allowed to refuse. Your job is to sit there.

— — —

It's windy out today. Lake Mjøsa is all white.
Sit here and watch the snow, and the wind
writing on it with invisible ink.
Breathe for a while. But not for too long. You have permission
to be happy. But only for little, little things.
And don't run away to the woods. We'll find you.

$\approx$

Men ennå har vi jo lov å tenke (mens øynene tygger og svelger)
at det er noe de gjemmer for oss. Noe de ikke vet ennå.
Bortenfor lydene og lyset. Sannheter
utenfor sannhetene.
Sånne som vinden skriver på sneen. For under sneen ligger jorden
og venter. Full av groe. Full av håp. Vet den mer
enn vi?

But in fact we can still manage to think (while our eyes chew and
    swallow)
that there's something they're hiding from us. Something they
    don't know yet.
Beyond the sounds and the light. Truths
beyond the truths.
Like the ones the wind writes on the snow. For under the snow the
    earth
lies waiting. Full of sprouts. Full of hope. Does it know
more than we do?

Kom igjen—

Dypt derinne,
bakenfor det tunge kneet mitt idag,
ligger et annet lite kne,
litt skittent og med skrubbsår på.
Og inne i fingrene mine, alle fem,
ligger en liten hånd, en annen,
ennå litt engstelig, men varm.
Og langt inne i skallen min,
helt innerst der,
kribler det av andre tanker,
rare og små, nesten med hyssing rundt, men de puster
ennå. Fulle av forventning, nesten av fryd.
Det hender det klør i dem—
de vil ut og leke
gjemsel med meg. Ofte—ofte.
Men da er de borte plutselig. Jeg finner
dem ikke igjen. Det er gått så mange år,
og blitt så mange svære lag av tid
utenpå alt.
———Men kom igjen da dere. Kom igjen,
så løper vi og gjemmer oss
alle, alle.

Come On—

Deep inside,
behind that heavy knee I've got today,
lies another, smaller knee,
a little dirty, and scraped.
And within my fingers, all five of them,
lies a small hand, another one,
still a bit anxious, but warm.
And far inside my skull,
in the innermost part,
other thoughts are tingling,
odd and small ones, almost wrapped up tight, but they're still
breathing. Full of expectation, almost of joy.
Sometimes they itch—
they want to come out and play
hide-and-seek with me. Often—often.
But then they're suddenly gone. I can't
find them again. So many years have passed,
so many heavy layers of time
have settled over everything.
— — —But come on back now. Come on,
let's run and hide,
every one, every one.

Se opp (OBS. OBS.)

Blir det sol på søndag?
Paraply på værkartet?
Vel, vel. Ditt problem.

Mitt er av et annet slag.
Kikk litt opp på skyene (engang du får tid).
De hører med til familien. Bor i annen etasje.
Og vi i første. Samme hus.

Og samme spørsmål. Noen
må ut og skure og vaske. Ofte natten lang.
Hustak og gater. Vanner rosenbed og dusjer
plenene til gartneren.
Noen dovner seg i solen. The Jet Set,
på luftmadrasser. Andre
bygger seg luksusboliger,
finere enn Ullernåsen. Hele slott
med tårn og takterrasser, swimmingpools
som provoserer til kanonbrak. Tordenbyger.
Glimt av ild,
til vinden rolig soper bort det hele.

Og noen blir trøtte av verden. Kei av alt.
Legger seg ned for å sove oppe i åsene.
Deprimerte. Ofte i dagevis.
Helt til solen kommer stikkende med sin sprøytespiss.
Da rusler de.

Og så har vi tåken. Skyene som tviler,
og går ned i gatene for å finne sannheten der.
Gjør de det?

Faktisk holder jeg meg mest til duskregnet
—sånn i det lange løp. Regnvær
er godt å jobbe i (for den som er innendørs).
Og det gjør jobben sin bra.
Vasker vinduet og utgangsdøren. Hele gaten.

Look Up (N.B. N.B.)

Will it be sunny on Sunday?
Umbrella on the weather map?
Well, then. Your problem.

Mine's of a different sort.
Take a peek up at the clouds (whenever you have time).
They're part of the family. Live on the second floor.
And we're on the first. Same house.

And the same issues. Somebody
has to go out and scrub and wash. Often all night.
Roofs and streets. Water rose beds and sprinkle
the gardener's lawns.
Some loaf in the sun. The Jet Set,
on air mattresses. Others
build luxurious villas for themselves,
finer than in Ullernåsen. Whole castles—
with towers and roof patios, swimming pools—
that provoke the crash of cannons. Thundershowers.
Flashes of fire
until the wind calmly sweeps it all away.

And some get tired of the world. Fed up with everything.
Lie down to sleep up in the hills.
Depressed. Often for days at a time.
Until the sun comes pricking with its hypodermic.
That rouses them.

And then we have the fog. Clouds that are in doubt
and go down into the streets to find the truth there.
Do they find it?

The fact is, I stick mostly to the drizzly days
—I mean for the long haul. Rainy weather
is good to work in (if you work indoors).
And it does its job well.
Washes the windows and the front door. The whole street.

Og gir gro-vann over alt det grønne. Hele jorden.
Alt det som vokser. Skogens trær og rug og ris og hvete.
Så jeg holder meg til det som ikke blender.
Skyslott og silkehimler. Pent å se på.
Men det holder ikke.
Gråværet
kan du stole på.

And waters all the greenery. The whole earth.
Everything that grows. The trees in the forest and wheat and rice
    and rye.
So I stick to what isn't dazzling.
Cloud-castles and silky skies—nice to look at.
But that's not enough.
Gray weather
is the kind you can trust.

I alle skoger har det bodd folk

Inne i alle skoger har det bodd folk.
De stirret mot skogbrynene. Og årene gikk fra dem.
De stirret mot skyene. Men det var så lite som hjalp.

Derfor er alle skogkantene vi har
så fulle av hakk i hakk,
nesten som sagblad, eller kanten på filleryer,
fryns i fryns.
De er slitt ned av alle vente-øynene
og lengte-blikkene
som så og så og så
om noen kom.

Og noen kom.
Men helst for sent.
De fleste kom ikke.
Bare vinteren kom, og høstregnet
og det hvite ansiktet under hoste-riene
kom. Men mest var det stilt,
og av og til bar de bort en kiste.

— — —

Fint å gå i skog, og helst i store.
Høre på susen der
og hva den brummer om med mørke stemmer.
Mummel-mummel, sier skogen.
Så langt av lei. Så langt av lei.
Men mere får du aldri vite,
aldri, aldri, aldri får du vite.

Og nå er det tomt snart
i husene i skogen.

In Every Forest

People have lived in every forest.
They stared at the borders of the forests. And the years left them.
They stared at the clouds. But there was so little that helped.

That's why the edges of all our woods
are ragged, notch after notch,
almost like ripsaws, or the ends of shag rugs,
fringe upon fringe.
They're worn down by all the waiting eyes
and longing glances
that looked and looked and looked
to see if anyone would come.

And some came.
But usually too late.
Most didn't come.
Only winter came, and the fall rain
and the white face during coughing fits
came. But mostly it was quiet,
and now and then they carried away a coffin.

— — —

Fine to walk in the forest, and best in a big one.
Listen to the rustling there
and what it's humming about with dark voices.
Mummel-mummel, says the forest.
So far away. So far away.
But more than that you'll never know—
you'll never, never, never get to know.

And soon there will be no one
dwelling in the forest.

Du fugl—

Du fugl i meg
—jeg kjenner vingen din.
Jeg kjenner nebbet hakke—hakke
mot sprinklene i brystet mitt. Jeg vet
du er en fange her.
Men vent
en liten stund.
Bare en liten stund,
så er du fri,
du fugl i meg.

You Bird—

You bird in me
—I feel your wing.
I feel your beak pecking—pecking
against the bars in my breast. I know
you are a prisoner here.
But wait
a little while.
Just a little while,
then you'll be free,
you bird in me.

Til deg

Tiden går (hva skal den ellers ta seg til).
En dag hører du den banke på døren din.
Den har banket på hos oss,
men jeg lukket ikke opp.
Ikke dennegang.

Vet du,
jeg har ofte stått og sett litt på deg,
sånn om morgenen foran speilet der
når du kjemmer håret ditt, det
knitrer i det, som i sne i påskefjellet
og du bøyer deg litt frem (jeg ser det godt)
—er det kommet en rynke til?
—Det er det ikke. For meg
er du ung.
Det er sevje i deg, skog. Et tre

og med fugler i. De synger ennå.
Kanskje litt lavt i høst, men likevel.
—Ikke en dag uten en latter i strupen,
eller det sakte streifet av en hånd.

En gang
må jeg holde den enda fastere,
for du vet, vi skal ut og reise snart,
og ikke med samme båt.
Noen har banket på døren vår, men gått igjen.
Dette
er visst det eneste vi aldri
har villet snakke om.

To You

Time moves along (what else would it be up to).
One day you hear it knocking on your door.
It knocked at our place,
but I didn't open up.
Not this time.

You know,
I've often stopped for a bit and watched you,
like in the morning in front of the mirror there
when you comb your hair, it
crackles, like snow in the mountains at Easter
and you bend forward a little (I see it clearly)
—I think that's another wrinkle.
—No it isn't. For me
you are young.
There is sap in you; forest. A tree

with birds in it. They still sing.
Perhaps a bit softly this autumn, but nonetheless.
—Not one day without a laugh in the throat
or the slow touch of a hand.

At some point
I'll have to hold it even tighter,
because, you know, we'll be traveling soon,
and not on the same boat.
Someone has knocked on our door, but gone away again.
Surely this
is the only thing we've never
wanted to talk about.

Om å sovne i en åker

Jeg kan huske jeg har sovnet i en åker, engang
da jeg var liten, fem-seks år og dum, engang,
og våknet av en frosk som satt på foten min
midt i en skog av grønnere enn grønt, engang.
Et tusenben kom krypende på hånden min,
og ør-små dyr jeg ikke kjente før, engang,
og kryp med underlige farver på
som kom og ville se hva dette var.
—En Gulliver i Lilleputters land, engang.
En snegl på kinnet mitt og maur i håret.
To markmus, de som har så blanke øyne
sto engstelig på vakt bak hvert sitt strå, engang.
Det var som i et hav, et verdensdyp, engang,
som ingen kjenner nå, men jeg fikk se, engang.
Og det jeg husker best var alt det duftet av.
—Av jord—som ligner jodlukt—og av alt som gror, engang.
Den stramme eim av sæd og gammel muld, engang,
og litt av kumøkk,
engang.

On Falling Asleep in a Field

I can remember falling asleep in a field, once
when I was little, five or six and dumb, once,
and waking 'cause a frog sat on my foot
in the middle of a forest greener than green, once.
A centipede came crawling onto my hand,
and tiny creatures I hadn't met before, once,
and insects that were wearing marvelous colors
and came to have a look at what this was.
—A Gulliver in a land of Lilliputians, once.
A snail-house on my cheek and ants in my hair.
A pair of field mice, the kind with shiny eyes,
stood anxious watch behind their blades of grass, once.
It was like an ocean deep beneath the world, once,
that no one knows about now, but I got to see, once.
And what I remember best is how much it smelled of.
—Of earth—which smells like iodine—and of everything that
    grows, once.
The pungent odor of semen and old humus, once,
and a whiff of cow dung,
once.

Bortafor Grorud—

Til Olav H. Hauge på 70-årsdagen

Det er ikke nødvendig
å bo i slike digre byer.
Det er ikke nødvendig
å rope høyt fra talerstoler
for å bli hørt.
Det er ikke nødvendig
stadig å tenke andres tanker
eller å snakke med andres munn.

Rart land, det her,
—bortafor Grorud.
Nordlys og nymåne
istedenfor gatelys.
Myrsørpe istedenfor fortauer.
Svupp—svupp sier det når du går
inn i de nye tidene, foran de fleste
som ikke kan se eller høre for motorbrølet,
neonflammene eller de skingrende stemmene.

Jeg er litt småsvak for de svære fjellene
der vest, islyset fra fonnene, og havet
som stikker fingrene inn her for å kjenne
om vi ennå er blant de levende,
—og for de store stillhetene—
(du får god hørsel av dem
og våre nerver). Du hører tingene
nesten før det er skjedd
—bortafor Grorud
eller Hakadal eller Sokna. Lese og lytte
og skrive ned. Slippe
å tenke andres tanker,
eller snakke med andres munn.

Beyond Grorud—
for Olav H. Hauge on his 70th birthday

It is not necessary
to live in such enormous cities.
It is not necessary
to shout from rostrums
in order to be heard.
It is not necessary
always to think others' thoughts
or to speak with others' mouths.

Strange country, around here,
—beyond Grorud.
Northern lights and new moon
instead of streetlights.
Marsh sludge instead of sidewalks.
Svurp—svurp it says when you walk
into the next age, ahead of the crowd,
who cannot see or hear for the roar of engines,
the neon flames or the piercing voices.

I have a weakness for those massive mountains
to the west, the icy light from the drifts, and the ocean
that sticks its fingers in here to feel
if we're still among the living,
—and for the great silences—
(you get good hearing from them,
and sharpened senses). You hear things
almost before they've happened
—beyond Grorud
or Hakadal or Sokna. Read and listen
and write it down. Escape
thinking others' thoughts,
and speaking with others' mouths.

Hundvåko

Hundvåko, Hangur og Skriulaupen.
Underlige navn vi har i dette landet vårt,
liksom hogd ut av berget, rett og slett,
eller skåret ut av gamle trestubber.

Men de svarer liksom ikke lenger til noe.
Vil kanskje ikke kjennes ved oss,
og ikke vi ved dem. Ikke motellene. Ikke bensinstasjonene,
og det vi snakker om eller tenker på.

Framrusthovdi, Uppnostindann', Tindulvstølane.
Det må ha bodd noen her før
som var mere kjente her enn vi er blitt,
og tok ordene rett ut av fjellveggen
og hogde dem til for oss som runer.
Holder det?

Hundvåko

Hundvåko, Hangur and Skriulaupen.
Peculiar names we have in this country of ours,
as if hacked out of the mountains, just as they are,
or chipped out of old tree stumps.

But it seems like they no longer fit anything.
Perhaps they're avoiding us,
and we them. Our motels. Our gas stations,
and what we talk or think about.

Framrusthovdi, Uppnostindann', Tindulvstølane.
People must have lived here before
who were familiar with the place in a way we've lost,
and took the words right out of the rock face
and carved them for us like runes.
Will they last?

Fjellregel

Det er den tynne sneen,
den som falt inatt,
som er så farlig, sier de.
Det ligger et islag under der
av gammel, forherdet sne. Det er den
som setter de store skredene igang
—de som river med seg alle.

Nysne, tynn, sprø
er falt inatt,
så trå ikke feil.
Husk på den gamle sneen,
den seige skorpen som ligger der og venter.
Så hold unna bratthenget.
Det kan begynne som en torden
og ende som en blinkende ljå.

Mountain Rule

It's the thin snow,
the kind that fell tonight,
that's so dangerous, they say.
Underneath it there's a layer of ice
made of old, hardened snow. That's what
sets off the big avalanches
—the ones that sweep everyone away.

Fresh snow, thin, crisp
has fallen tonight,
so don't miss a step.
Remember the old snow,
the tough crust is lying in wait.
So stay away from the steep slope.
It can start like a thunderclap
and end as a flashing scythe.

—Mere fjell

Av og til
må noe vare lenge,
ellers mister vi vel vettet snart,
så fort som allting snurrer rundt med oss.
Store trær er fint
og riktig gamle hus er fint,
men enda bedre—
fjell.
Som ikke flytter seg en tomme
om hele verden enn forandres
(og det må den snart),
så står de der
og står og står
så du har noe å legge pannen inntil,
og kjøle deg
og holde i noe fast.

Jeg trivs med fjell.
De lager horisonter
med store hugg i,
som de var smidd av smeder.
Tenk på: — Den gamle nupen her har stått som nå
helt siden Haralds-tiden.
Den sto her da de spikret en arming fast til korset.
Som nå. Som nå.
Med sildrebekker på og lyngkjerr og den store
bratte pannen
uten tanker i. Den sto her
under Belsen og Hiroshima. Den står her nå
som landemerke for din død, din uro,
kanskje dine håp.
Så du kan gå derbort og holde i noe hardt.
Noe gammelt noe. Som stjernene.
Og kjøle pannen din på den,
og tenke tanken ut.
Og tenke selv.

—More Mountains

Here and there
something must endure,
or soon we'll surely lose our wits,
things have got us whirling around so fast.
Large trees are fine
and really old houses are fine,
but even better—
mountains.
Which won't budge an inch
even if the whole world is changed
(as it soon must be);
they'll stand there
and stand and stand
so you can lay your forehead against something,
and cool yourself
and hold onto something solid.

I like mountains.
They make horizons
with big notches,
as if they were forged by smiths.
Think of it: — That old round-top has stood as it stands now
all the time since King Harald's day.
It stood here when they nailed a poor wretch to the cross.
As it stands now. As it stands now.
Wearing trickling streams and heather scrub and that large
steep brow
without any thoughts in it. It stood here
through Belsen and Hiroshima. It stands here now
as a landmark for your death, your unease,
perhaps your hopes.
So you can go over there and hold onto something hard.
Some old something. Like the stars.
And cool your forehead on it,
and think your thoughts through.
And think for yourself.

Klokkene fra Assisi

Hør klokkeklangene fra Assisi ved morgengry.
De flyr som fugleflokker, høyt mot himlen over Umbria.
«Vi finner dem — Vi finner dem — Vi finner dem.»

Hør klokketonene fra Assisi ved aftentid,
når de som trette fugleskarer vender hjem igjen:
«Vi fant dem ikke — fant dem ikke — fant dem ikke.»

—Ikke EN som ville skjenke oss sin kappe.
—Ikke EN som ville legge ned sitt sverd.

The Bells from Assisi

Hear the peals of the bells from Assisi at daybreak.
They fly like birds, high against the heavens over Umbria.
"We'll find them — We'll find them — We'll find them."

Hear the notes of the bells from Assisi in the evening,
when like tired flocks of birds they turn back home:
"We couldn't find them — couldn't find them — couldn't
    find them."

—Not ONE who would offer us his cloak.
—Not ONE who would lay down his sword.

«Silvery Moon»

Hva gjør du i downtown, Kansas City (Mo.) om kvelden
når det plutselig dukker opp en diger flod foran øynene dine
med en bru av måneskinn tvers over møkkavannet, nesten som
Hollywood, og du sitter på en støpejernsbenk i Kersey Coates,
midt under pengetårnene?

Du blir sittende bare og kope, selvfølgelig
(og vente på at noen skal slå deg ned, eller i alle fall
bomme deg for en sigarett).

Joda. Han kom. Og han fikk sin røyk.
I am an artist myself (have been), he said.
I am a painter.
Og du sitter her og myser på denne månen vår.
Slutt nå med det. We've been there, you know.
Det er bare aske og sand. Sånn som med oss.
Glitter og stas
lager vi bedre selv. Nei, sola du.
Sola. Sånn som van Gogh.
Og menneskene— —
sånn som de er.
Men si meg en ting,
(Har du en blås til). Jeg har spurt meg selv
—Hvordan kan det ha seg
at vi snart vet mere om månen idag
enn om menneskene?

Ser du vestover der.
Der kommer Kansas River (Dodge City, you know it?)
og her kommer Missouri, bak søppeltomtene derborte.
Har du sett no så stygt som her.
To floder—mektige—som møtes.
Og så blir det dette.
—Nei, jeg får vel rusle. Jobbe litt ikveld.
Må jo leve

"Silvery Moon"

What do you do in downtown Kansas City (Mo.) at night
when an enormous river suddenly appears before your eyes
with a bridge of moonlight straight across the filthy water, almost
    like
Hollywood, and you're sitting on a cast-iron bench in Kersey
    Coates,
right below the money towers?

You just keep gaping, obviously
(and expecting someone to mug you, or at least
bum a cigarette).

Yessir. He came. And he got his smoke.
I am an artist myself (have been), he said.
I am a painter.
And you're sitting here squinting at this moon of ours.
Well quit it. *We've been there, you know.*
It's only ashes and sand. Just like down here.
As for glitter and flash
we do that better ourselves. Nah, the sun's the thing, you know.
The sun. Like in Van Gogh.
And people— —
such as they are.
But tell me something
(Have you got another smoke). I've asked myself
—How is it that one of these days
we're gonna know more about the moon
than about people?

Look west there.
That's the Kansas River *(Dodge City, you know it?)*
and here comes the Missouri, behind those empty lots full
    of rubbish.
Ever seen a place so ugly?
Two rivers—huge ones—that meet.
And we end up with this.
—Well, I guess I'll get going. Work a little tonight.
Gotta live

etpar år til iallfall, så vi får se
om det går til helvete med alt,
som noen sier.
Om du vil vite det så er jeg født i Tulsa,
Arkansas River—samme styggedommen der.

Ja, som jeg sa deg, broder.
Jeg driver og maler litt, men bare tant og flitter.
Alt sånt som smiler,—helt til øra.
Folk som er sinnssykt glade både dag og natt.
Ansikter uten rynker, juks og svindel.
Sannheten er de redd for. Tårer
selger ikke. Ikke for meg.
Det er jeg som drysser sølvpengene over elva
og lager skyer sånn som ikveld, med gullkant på.
Så nå skjønner du vel (En fyrstikk, Mister)
at det er jeg som er månen,
så nå kan du si at du så meg full
og fager i Kansas City, Terrace Park,
downtown i Kersey Coates.

a couple of more years anyway, so we can see
if everything goes up in smoke
like some people say.
In case you want to know, I was born in Tulsa,
Arkansas River—same awfulness there too.

Yeah, like I said, brother.
I do a little painting—but only worthless crap.
Everything smiling—from ear to ear.
People who're insanely happy day and night.
Faces without wrinkles, lying junk.
They're afraid of the truth. Tears
don't sell. Not for me.
I'm the one who scatters the silver coins over the river
and makes clouds like tonight, with gilt edges.
So now you understand, I guess (Another match, mister?)
that the moon is me,
and now you can say that you saw me lit up
and handsome in Kansas City, Terrace Park,
downtown in Kersey Coates.

Inlandsbanan
(Gällivare – Östersund, tog 4679)

Det går et tog for kanonenes skyld
gjennom det innerste av Skandinavia.
Jeg så bautaen over de første falne,
de som ikke sprang fort nok da mineskuddene smalt,
og det var mange. Men nesten ingen idag
stiger av eller på
ved Kåbdalis, Moskosel eller Koosakåbbå,
stasjoner som dør snart, de har ingen vinduer mer,
så her er det stopp bare for dyrene, elgerumper
i ny og ne, en tiur i sporet, og flokken av reinsdyr
som ikke vil rikke seg. De har tid nok.

For mennesket bor ikke her. «Evakuering»
sa skrivebordsfolket. Nå bor de i kjøpegatene
og stappes med leketøy så de tier.
Utdødde smågrender haster forbi. Likhauger av hus,
og en stripe av asfalt
som viser veien til kirkegården.

Men nordlyset lever ennå. Blafrende som gardiner.
Noen har åpnet et himmelvindu her. Det flagrer i blått og grønt
ut mot et ukjent rom. — Klar til evakuering
også her?
Nye stasjoner, halvdøde av sult:
Vargtandberget, Vojmån og Vilhelmina.
Store elver Lule, Pite og Ume
på sterke broer, spent over for troppetogenes skyld,
skjønt det sitrer i dem som hos redde soldater
for farten er stor, 110 – 120. Ved Ulriksfors
kommer en tant ombord med kaffe och tidningar,
og med øynene stappet fulle av terror og voldtekter,
kvinnepupper og krig, kjører vi inn på Östersund Central
spor fire, 21,23 presis efter ruten.

The Inland Line

(Gällivare – Östersund, Sweden, train 4679)

For the sake of the cannons there is a train
that runs through the heart of Scandinavia.
I saw the rough stone monument
raised over the first to fall,
the ones who didn't run fast enough when the blasting charges
    went off,
and there were many. But today almost no one
gets on or off
at Kåbdalis, Moskosel or Koosakåbbå,
stations that will die soon, they have no windows anymore,
so these are stops only for the animals, moose rumps
now and then, a wood grouse on the tracks, and a herd of reindeer
that won't budge. They have time enough.

For people don't live here. "Evacuation"
said the paper-pushers. Now they live in the shopping malls
and get drowned in toys so they'll keep quiet.
Extinct villages rush by. Mounds of cadaverous houses,
and a strip of asphalt
that shows the way to the graveyard.

But the northern lights are still alive. Fluttering like curtains.
Someone has opened a window in the sky here. Blue and green
flap out toward uncharted space. — Ready for evacuation
here too?
New stations, half starved to death:
Vargtandberget, Vojmån and Vilhelmina.
Across big rivers, the Lule, the Pite and the Ume,
on strong bridges, built for the troop trains
—but they tremble like frightened soldiers,
for the speed is high, 110 – 120. At Ulriksfors
a matron comes aboard with "coffee and papers";
and with eyes jammed full of terrorism and rapes,
women's breasts and war, we ride into Östersund Central,
track four, 9:23 P.M., exactly on time.

fra NATTÅPENT
≈ ≈ ≈ ≈ ≈

1985

from NIGHT WATCH

≈ ≈ ≈ ≈ ≈

1985

HALVVEIS
BARE HALVVEIS
VIL VI SANNE TANKENE VÅRE.
HALVVEIS, BARE HALVVEIS
ER ORDENE LIVET BARE
HALVVEIS HAR JEG LEVD.
HALVVEIS ER DØDEN, VERDEN
I ØYNENE VÅRE OG DYPERE
KOMMER DU IKKE.

PART WAY
WE WILL CONFIRM
OUR THOUGHTS ONLY PART WAY.
PART WAY, ONLY PART WAY
OUR WORDS OUR LIFE IT'S ONLY
PART WAY I'VE LIVED.
DEATH AND THE WORLD IN OUR EYES
PART WAY AND DEEPER THAN THAT
YOU WON'T GET.

Trær om høsten

—når de har mistet sommeren sin
kan vi gå ut og se hva de er gjort av.
Årenettet, bærebjelkene,
styrke eller tafatthet, ben eller brusk.
Forsvarsløse. Nå
gjennemskuer vi dem.

Trees in Autumn

—when the summer's gone out of them
we can see what they're made of.
The vesseled maze, the spreading beams,
strength or helplessness, bone or cartilage.
Defenseless. Now
we see through them.

Tanker ved Sjodalsvatn

Var det lur-tonen fra alle fossene her
som engang lærte skaldene å kvede
og fødte ordene i Håvamål og trollet i eventyrene?
I ingen land jeg vet om
hørtes så mange horn og harper.
I alle daler, utfor alle skrenter
toner det helt inn i tinningene
av vann som synger, kaller,
lokker deg til drømmer.

Nå er det meste lagt i rør
og mangt er borte, men det må være slik
som det må gå med deg og meg:
Noe må temmes ned og bli til kraft og ånd
men noe må flomme fritt
sånn som sangen fra Gjendeoset borti her
og i blodet vårt,
den som forynger verden.

Thoughts at Lake Sjodal

Was it the mountain-horn played by the waterfalls
that once taught the skalds how to sing
and gave birth to the words in *Hávamál*
and put magic in the stories of trolls?
No country I know of
has heard so many woodwinds and harps.
In every valley, down every cliff
the notes go ringing through your temples—
water that sings and calls and
lures you to dreams.

Now most of it's been run into pipes
so the music is gone, but I guess
it's just like with us:
Something's got to be tamed and turned into power and spirit
but something's got to flow free,
like the song from the Gjende Rapids over there
and in our blood,
the one that rejuvenates the world.

Plutselig. I desember

Plutselig. I desember. Jeg står til knes i sne.
Snakker med deg og får ikke svar. Du tier.
Elskede, så er det altså hendt. Hele livet vårt,
smilet, tårene og motet. Symaskinen din
og alle arbeidsnettene. Reisene våre tilslutt:
  —under sneen. Under den brune kransen.

Alt gikk så fort. To stirrende øyne. Ord
jeg ikke forsto, som du gjentok og gjentok.
Og plutselig ingenting mer. Du sov.
Og nå ligger de her. Alle dagene, sommernettene,
druene i Valladolid, solnedgangene i Nemi
  —under sneen. Under den brune kransen.

Lynsnart som når en bryter slås av
blir alle billedsporene bak øyet tonet ned,
visket ut av livets tavle. Eller blir de ikke?
Den nye kjolen din, ansiktet mitt og trappen vår
og alt du bar til huset. Er det borte
  —under sneen. Under den brune kransen?

Kjæreste venn, hvor er vår glede nu,
de gode hendene, det unge smilet,
hårets lyskrans over pannen din og disse
pikelige glimt i øyet, ditt mot, og
dette overskudd av liv og håp?
  —Under sneen. Under den brune kransen.

Kamerat bak døden. Ta meg ned til deg.
Side ved side. La oss se det ukjente.
Her er så ødslig nu og tiden mørkner.
Ordene blir så få og ingen hører mer.
Kjæreste, du som sover. Evrydike.
  —Under sneen. Under den brune kransen.

Suddenly. In December

Suddenly. In December. I stand knee-deep in snow.
Talk to you and get no answer. You're keeping quiet.
My love, now it's happened after all. Our whole life,
the smiles, the tears and the courage. Your sewing machine
and the long nights of work. Finally our travels:
     —under the snow. Under the wreath of cedar.

It all went so fast. Two staring eyes. Words
I couldn't catch, that you said over and over.
And suddenly nothing more. You slept.
And now they're all lying here, days and summer nights,
the grapes in Valladolid, the sunsets in Nemea
     —under the snow. Under the wreath of cedar.

Quick as a switch flicking off,
the tracings behind the eye flash out,
wiped from the slate of a life-span. Or maybe not?
Your new dress, my face and our old stairs
and everything you brought to this house. Is it gone
     —under the snow. Under the wreath of cedar?

Dear friend, where is our happiness now,
your good hands, your young smile,
your hair's wreath of light on your forehead and that
girlish glint in your eye, your spirit and
steady abundance of life and hope?
     —Under the snow. Under the wreath of cedar.

Companion beyond death. Take me down with you.
Side by side, let us see the unknown.
It's so desolate here and the days are growing dark.
The words are few now and no one's listening anymore.
Dearest, you who are sleeping. Eurydice.
     —Under the snow. Under the wreath of cedar.

Rom 301

—Ja, nå kan De få komme inn.
De hadde kledt deg i hvitt.
Jeg tok den unge hånden din i min en stund.
Den svarte ikke. Aldri mer.
Den som strøk meg så ofte over håret,
nå siden sommeren. Helt fra pannen
ned i nakken. Som om du søkte
efter noe eller visste noe.
Visste du?

(Hånden din, lille hånden din.)
Den andre har de lagt på brystet ditt
bøyet om en rose. Rødt mot hvitt. En brud
men ikke min.
Så er tiden ute. Noen venter.
(Ansiktet, pannen, hendene.)
Jeg går mot døren,
nordlyset, stjernevrimlen,
ta imot.

Hånden på dørhåndtaket.
Det lille kneppet tilslutt.
Skrittene i korridoren. Klipp-klapp
klipp-klapp. Slik
ender et liv.

Room 301

—All right, you may come in now.
They had dressed you in white.
I held your young hand for a time.
It didn't respond. Never again.
The hand that so often stroked my hair
lately, since the summer. All the way
from my forehead to my neck. As if you were looking
for something or knew something.
Did you know?

(Your hand, your small hand.)
The other one they've laid on your breast,
curved around a rose. Red on white. A bride
but not mine.
Then the time is up. Someone's waiting.
(Face, forehead, hands.)
I walk toward the door;
northern lights, swarm of stars—
be open.

Hand on the doorknob.
The final little click.
Steps in the corridor. Clip-clop
clip-clop. That's how
a life ends.

Piggtrådvinter

— —Ho.
Da vi giftet oss da var det kaldt, da.
Minst femogtjue harde,
solvervsdag, nittenførr,
krig og kvegpest.
Veien til kjerka var stengt med piggtråd.
Husker vi klatret over skigarden til prestegarden.
—Hei, kjolen din henger fast,
—nei ikke der men der.
Vi tråtte plogfurer over en is-klaka
potetåker opp til presten i serk
som sto klar med skriften.
—*Jag* efter kjærligheten, sa'n. Ja, sa vi.
Men du verden hvor møkkete vi var på bena.
Da vi hadde lagt oss om kvelden
grein vi en skvett, begge to. Gud
vet hvorfor.
Og så begynte det lange livet.

Barbed-wire Winter

— —Boy!
When we got married—now, that was cold weather.
At least twenty-five below,
winter solstice, nineteen-forty,
war and rinderpest.
Road to the church was blocked with barbed wire.
I remember we clambered over the rail fence of the parsonage.
—Hey, your dress is caught
—no, not there—over there.
We tramped the furrows of an ice-crusted
potato field, up to the minister
who was in his surplice and had
the Scriptures ready.
—Love is a *path* you must walk, he says. Yes, we said.
But my lord what muddy feet we had!
When we got in bed that night
we cried a dab—both of us. God
knows why.
And then the long life began.

Symaskinen

Lyst hode over en symaskin,
dypere og dypere ned. Nå sovner hun
oppå den gule kjolen
som skulle vært ferdig nå.
Morgensolen fanger inn en saks
og tre stumper av snelletråd.
Liten gutt kommer lydløst inn en dør:
—Hun sover.
Og stemmen hennes: Å
—jeg sovnet visst.
To øyne mot meg prøvde et smil.
—Har bare littegran igjen.

Nå har du ingenting igjen.
Ikke til fredag, ikke til lørdag
og ingenting som haster mer
hverken for deg eller meg.

The Sewing Machine

A fair head over a sewing machine,
further and further down. And she falls asleep
right on the yellow dress
that was supposed to be finished by now.
The morning sun creeps onto a pair of scissors
and three short ends of thread.
Silently a small boy comes through a door:
—She's asleep.
And her voice: Oh
—I must have dozed off.
Two eyes turned toward me and tried a smile.
—I've just got a little bit left.

Now you've got nothing left.
Not due Friday, not due Saturday
and there's nothing urgent anymore,
not for you or for me.

Kjente jeg deg?

Kjente jeg deg
egentlig. Noe
du aldri fikk sagt eller
vi lot ligge. Halv-
tenkte tanker. En skygge
som strøk over ansiktet.
Noe i øynene. Nei
jeg vil ikke tro det.
Men det kommer igjen. Natten
har ingen lyd,
bare rare tanker. Ord
som stiger opp av søvnen:
Kjente jeg deg?

Did I Know You?

Did I know you
really. Things
you never quite said or
we let lie. Half-thought
thoughts. A shadow
that passed over your face.
Something in your eyes. No,
I don't want to believe that.
But it comes back. Night
has no sounds,
only strange thoughts. Words
that rise up from my sleep:
Did I know you?

Det var her—

Det var her. Akkurat her
ved bekken og det gamle nypekjerret.
Sen vår iår, rosene er bleke ennå,
nesten som kinnet ditt
den første morgenen bak døden.
Men det kommer,
bare lyset, bare duften, bare gleden
kommer ikke.

Men det var her
og det var kveld og måne,
bekkesildr
sånn som nå. Ta hånden min,
legg armen der.
Så går vi da
sammen i sommernatten, tause
mot det som
ikke er.

It Was Here—

It was here. Right here
beside the brook and the old rosebush.
A late spring this year, the roses are still pale,
almost like your cheek
the first morning beyond death.
But it's coming,
only the light, only the fragrance, only the pleasure
won't be coming.

But it was here,
it was an evening with a moon,
the brook trickling,
like now. Take my hand,
put your arm there.
And we'll set out
together in the summer night,
silently, toward
what isn't.

Ildfluene

Det var den aftenen med ildfluene
da vi sto og ventet på bussen til Velletri
at vi så de to gamle som sto og kysset hverandre
under platantreet. Det var da
du sa, halvt ut i luften
halvt til meg:
Den som har elsket lenge
har ikke levd forgjeves.
Og det var da jeg fikk øye på de første
ildfluene i mørket, knitrende
med lysblink rundt hodet ditt.
Det var da.

Fireflies

It was that evening with the fireflies
as we were waiting for the bus to Velletri
that we saw two old people kissing
under the plane tree. It was then
you said, half to the air
half to me:
Whoever loves for years
hasn't lived in vain.
And it was then I caught sight of the first
fireflies in the darkness, sparkling
with flashes of light around your head.
It was then.

ET SISTE DIKT
≈ ≈ ≈ ≈ ≈

A Last Poem

≈ ≈ ≈ ≈ ≈

Et dikt om elven Glåma

Storelven Glåma nord i verden.
Brei som et stuegulv under stjernene.
Kommer fra skogene. Først i Solør
blir den en flod like brei som Donau.

Her i det gamle fattiglandet
la den et håpets bånd, det blåe,
ventet på tiden, ventet på tankene
til vi kom inn i en ny slags verden.

Her var min barndom—barføtt-tiden.
Nå er jeg gammel og ser tilbake
—sanden på Lauta. — Lykkestunder
tett ved det blinkende blåe vannspeilet.

Strandsjøer, dauvann og dype sandbrått.
Tidevervselven som speiler stjernene,
himlenes regnvær og solgangsskyene.
Bakenfor tanken vår har vi deg med oss.

(juni 1992)

A Poem on the River Glåma

The great river Glåma, north in the world.
Broad as a ballroom floor beneath the stars.
Flows from the forests. Passing Solør
it becomes a watercourse wide as the Danube.

Here in the old peasant country
it put down a band of hope, a blue one,
bided its time, collected its thoughts
until we entered a new sort of world.

My childhood was here—barefoot-days.
Now I'm old and look back
—the beach at Lauta. — Happy times
close to the flashing blue mirror of water.

Sandbars, and still water in deep pools.
River of Ages that reflects the stars,
gray-weather skies and sun-steered clouds.
Behind our thoughts, we know you are with us.

(June 1992)

Notes

Some of the information in these notes was provided by Rolf Jacobsen. For biographical details I have often relied on Hanne Lillebo's *Ord må en omvei: En biografi om Rolf Jacobsen* (Oslo: Aschehoug, 1998). The Norwegian Language Council has provided some historical information about Norwegian orthography.

The pronunciations given here are approximations only. Note that "ò" here stands for the pure *o* sound of French, Spanish, or German, rather than for the English *aw* sound of *hawk*. A superscript *y* indicates that the tongue is held in position for initial *y* (as in *yes*) while the *preceding* sound is pronounced.

In notes about the Norwegian texts, I refer by their Norwegian titles to the twelve individual volumes of poetry that Jacobsen published (see the table of contents) and by abbreviation to the following editions, all of which except *TSA* were published in Oslo by Gyldendal Norsk Forlag:

> *DU: Dikt i utvalg* [Selected Poems], ed. Asbjørn Aarnes and Emil Boyson (1967)
> *SD 1973: Samlede dikt* [Collected Poems], "Lanterne" paperback edition (1973)
> *SD 1977: Samlede dikt* (1977)
> *SD 1982: Samlede dikt* (1982)
> *TSA: The Silence Afterwards: Selected Poems of Rolf Jacobsen*, trans. and ed. Roger Greenwald (Princeton University Press, 1985)
> *SD 1986: Samlede dikt*, "De nye klassikerne" paperback edition (1986)
> *AMD: Alle mine dikt* [All My Poems], ed. Sigmund Moren (1990)
> *SD 1999: Samlede dikt*, ed. Hanne Lillebo (1999)

(The last of these reproduces, with minor exceptions, the texts of the first editions of Jacobsen's twelve individual volumes. For a general discussion of the above editions, see the section called "The Text" in the introduction.)

Marshes   *p. 7*
This poem was deleted from *AMD*.

The Clouds   *p. 9*
This poem was deleted from *AMD*.

Plate Glass   *p. 15*
"As we left a blue wake behind us . . ." The blueness of the wavy reflections is not just the poet's fancy. There have been blue trolleys in Oslo since 1894, and

blue became the color of the entire fleet within a year or two after 1924, when the municipality acquired all privately owned lines.

Metaphysics of the City   *p. 17*

In the first edition of *Jord og jern,* a page division fell after the first two lines of stanza 4. Probably as a result of this accidental division, *SD 1973* inserted a blank line at this point, thus dividing the stanza into two. *SD 1977, 1982,* and *1986,* as well as *TSA* and *AMD,* repeat the blank line, which the logic of the poem suggests should not be there. In reproducing the layout of the first editions, Lillebo removes the blank line in *SD 1999.* Although, unlike her, I have in general followed later editions in order to incorporate intentional revisions, in this case I too have preferred the first edition and removed the blank line, since I regard it as the result of an oversight.

Railroad Country   *p. 21*

The Norwegian word *boggi* is taken from the British word *bogie,* which denotes both a four-wheeled truck that can swivel in relation to the railroad car mounted on it, and a car mounted on such a truck. *Brekkvogn* now means "baggage car" but once referred to freight cars as well; *brekk* simply means "brake."

Hjerpetjerns-hovet ['yar-pe-ˌshʸarns-'hȯ-ve]: a tunnel (named for the mountain it passes through) that was opened for traffic on the Southern Line of the Norwegian State Railway at about the time this poem was written.

Rubber   *p. 35*

The word *landeveiene* in line 2 has no exact equivalent in American English. These are the roads one drives on to travel long distances through Norway, but in the 1930s most of them were nothing like American highways. Even now they rarely have more than one lane in each direction and almost never have overpasses or cloverleaf interchanges (traffic circles are more common). As the poem makes clear, such roads sometimes traverse long stretches of forest. Therefore the associations evoked by "country roads" are roughly correct, but the Norwegian roads meant here are not short or winding rural ones; they are more like some of the older interstate highways in wooded areas of the United States.

The brand name of tire originally used by Jacobsen in line 6 was "Kelly." In his 1977 translation of this poem, Robert Bly used "Firestone." Working in the early 1980s, I preferred "Goodyear"; Jacobsen amiably went along with updating the brand name.

Heredity and Environment   *p. 39*

In the first edition of *Vrimmel,* a page division falls after line 6 of the second stanza. In *SD 1973* a blank line appears at this point; it also appears in *SD 1977, 1982,* and *1986,* as well as in *AMD. SD 1999* removes the blank line, so that the poem has two stanzas rather than three. In response to questions about typography that I sent him on 13 May 1985, Jacobsen confirmed that he wished to have the stanza break, so I retained it in *TSA* and have done so here as well.

Coke   *p. 47*

Oslo was known as Christiania from 1624 to 1877, and as Kristiania [ˌkris-tē-ˈän-ē-ä] from 1877 to 1924, when the original name of the city on that site was restored. Teatergaten (Theater Street) is in the downtown area of the city; it is where the Jacobsen family was living when Rolf Jacobsen was born.

Cobalt   *p. 49*

In the first edition of *Fjerntog,* and in *DU* and *SD 1973,* the last line of this poem is indented. The indention disappears in later editions of *SD.* In response to questions I sent him in February 1983, Jacobsen confirmed that he wished to retain the indention.

Express Train   *p. 53*

The layout of this poem has a checkered history; there are scarcely two editions of Jacobsen's work in which the poem appears in the same form. In the last edition of his work that Jacobsen supervised *(AMD)* he is still struggling to divide the first part of the poem into verse lines. Because I heard prose rhythms in all the text before the line that begins "Hva ville stige høyere her enn fjellene" ("What would rise higher here than the mountains"), and because this part of the text seemed in several editions merely to break when it filled the measure, I asked Jacobsen if he had intended it as prose. He said yes, and he referred to the first part of the poem as the prose section in notes he made on the galley proofs of *TSA.* (Evidently he had other intentions later, but I think both the language itself and the layout in the first edition of *Fjerntog* support setting the first part of the poem as prose.) Division of the prose passage into two paragraphs was a new revision by Jacobsen for *TSA.*

For *boggi,* see the note to "Railroad Country."

The Skarvang ['skär-ˌväŋ] Hills: a fictitious place name.

Marnardal ['mär-när-ˌdäl]: a town and railroad station in West Agder County, about 20 miles (30 km) west of Kristiansand.

In the Varald Forest   *p. 59*

The Varald ['vä-ˌräl] Forest is in Hedmark County, on the Swedish border, about 15 miles (25 km) east of Kongsvinger and 60 miles (100 km) east of Oslo. Varildbakken, or Varild Hill, is a small settlement south of the forest.

Lebbikø ['le-bik-ˌœ], Jakobsbakken ['yä-kòbs-ˌbäkᵊn], Sarjalampi ['sär-yä-ˌläm-pē], and Vais [vaēs] all lie nearby in Finnskogene, or the Finns' Forests, an area populated by Finnish immigrants from about 1600 onward.

The Valley of Gudbrandsdal ['gūͤd-bräns-ˌdäl] is a large valley renowned for its beauty. It runs northwest from Lillehammer. Grip [grēp] is a group of tiny islands in Møre and Romsdal County, about 10 miles (15 km) north of Kristian-sund. A lighthouse there bears the same name.

North Fosen ['fü-s³n], Bykle-hei ['bʉk-le-'haē], Kvindegardslii ['kvin-e-ˌgärs-'lē-yē], Vinje ['vin-ye]: The place names are meant to convey Norway's large extent and varied geographical character.

Pavane *p. 65*

The pavane, a stately Spanish dance of the 16th and 17th centuries, is "said to be so called because in it the dancers stalked like peacocks (Latin *pavones*), the gentlemen with their long robes of office, and the ladies with trains like peacocks' tails. The pavan[e], like the minuet, ended with a quick movement called the *galliard,* a sort of gavotte" (*Brewer's Dictionary of Phrase and Fable* [London: Cassell, 1963]).

Landscape with Steam Shovels *p. 67*

For thematic reasons, in Norway this became (with the help of schoolbooks) one of Jacobsen's best-known poems. My estimation of it rose when I discovered a biblical allusion that I felt added considerable resonance. Its description of the steam shovels would seem to refer to the description of heathen idols ("the work of men's hands") in Psalm 115:5–8: "They have mouths, but they speak not: eyes have they, but they see not . . . feet have they, but they walk not: neither speak they through their throat." The psalmist comments: "They that make them are like unto them; so is every one that trusteth in them."

I have emended "ekshaust" in the Norwegian text to "exhaust," since the spelling with *ks* in *Hemmelig liv* seems to conform to a spelling reform that Jacobsen had not in fact adopted. As late as in "Fasten your seat belts—" (*Tenk på noe annet,* 1979), Jacobsen writes "galaxer" rather than "galakser."

The Age of the Great Symphonies *p. 69*

Villabyene means "the cities of private houses" and contrasts with *murstenshavet,* "the sea of brick"—older apartment buildings in the centers of cities.

"Seid umschlungen Millionen" ['zaēd üm-'shluŋ-en mi-lē-'ö-nen] is a phrase from Schiller's "An die Freude" (in English commonly known as "Ode to Joy"), the poem that provided the text for the last movement of Beethoven's Ninth Symphony (1823). It means "Be embraced, you millions."

The Archaeologist *p. 73*

The lines in Old Norse (italicized) are a transcription of the first sentence of the inscription on the Eggjum Stone, Norway's most famous rune stone, which dates from slightly before 700 A.D. They mean, approximately, "The stone is not sought by sun nor cut by knife [*or* sword]." There has been considerable debate among scholars about the sentence's exact lexical content and its intended meaning. Some, referring to well-known beliefs that exposure to sunlight and contact with iron vitiate magical powers, hold that the sentence attests to the way the inscription was made. Others read the sentence as an invocation against grave robbers.

Blommenholm ['blȯm-en-ˌhȯlm]: a suburb and railway stop west of Oslo.

Timber   *p. 75*

Ångermanelven, the Ångerman ['ȯŋ-er-män] River, flows south and southeast across Sweden and empties into the Gulf of Bothnia (at about 63° N) just past Kramfors, which is the center for the area's lumber-based industry.

Deep Creek, British Columbia, is the name of a small settlement 40 miles (65 km) east of Kamloops and of a river that arises nearby and flows south for about 20 miles (30 km) into Okanagan Lake.

In stanza 4, most Norwegian editions print the second line as a long one that does not break until after "kommer av," so that the third line has only two words, "stor kjærlighet." However, *DU* breaks the second line after "viljen i sig." In response to questions I sent him on 26 December 1982, Jacobsen indicated that he preferred this line break, so I retained it in *TSA* and have done so here as well.

It is clear in the first edition of *Hemmelig liv* that the next-to-last stanza of this poem consists of three lines; the last of these is quite long, and the end of it, the phrase "som minner om dans," is printed near the right margin as a runover. In all later Norwegian editions of Jacobsen's work except *SD 1999*, the runover phrase moves to the left margin and thereby becomes a separate line. Jacobsen confirmed in writing in May 1985 that this change was an error; in the same month he corrected the error on the galley proofs of *TSA*. I therefore treated the third line in the stanza as one long line in *TSA* and have done so here as well.

Rolf Jacobsen wrote on the galley proofs of *TSA* that he wanted stress to fall on the word *tømmer* (timber) in the last sentence of this poem, but was unsure how to achieve this. He later told me that he wanted a pause after this word. The first edition of *Hemmelig liv* prints the last clause of the sentence on a separate but indented line. In *TSA* I retained the indention to try to indicate a pause, but the result was probably mistaken for the runover of a long line, so I have removed the indention here. Lillebo concludes that the last sentence was probably originally intended as one long verse line. That is a reasonable conclusion (though impossible to confirm), but in this case I am persuaded that the later printing of the last clause as a separate, third line in the final stanza was intentional. (Jacobsen wrote to me that he could not remember in this instance whether he had made the change intentionally.)

Turnip Crop   *p. 87*

Huitzilopochtli [ˌwē-tsē-lō-'pōch-tlē] was a warrior god, the mythic leader and chief divinity of the Aztecs. His name means "Hummingbird of the South"; he may have been a god of the southern sun. His temple, in the center of Tenochtitlán, was the object of a famous battle with Cortez and his men in 1520; it was razed after the Conquest.

All the Norwegian editions use an unofficial, pronunciation-based spelling, "Vitsilopechtli," that Jacobsen wrote from memory; I have corrected the *e* to an *o*, but have retained the spelling "Vitsi-" in the Norwegian text, since it is likely that Jacobsen adopted it intentionally to help his Norwegian readers pronounce the name.

Meadowsweet   *p. 89*
This poem was deleted from *AMD*.

Mournful Towers   *p. 91*
In the first edition of *Hemmelig liv* and in *DU* there is no stanza break in this poem. In *SD 1973*, a page division falls after the third line. *SD 1977, 1982,* and *1986,* as well as *TSA* and *AMD,* insert a blank line at that point. Although the shift from past tense to present makes the stanza break look plausible, the available evidence supports Lillebo's conclusion that the break is spurious; I have therefore eliminated it here.

In line 3 of the Norwegian, a *stenhammer* is a rounded outcropping of rock that protrudes from a cliff or rock face. Jacobsen's image pictures the slaves' shoulders as cliffs and their hands, lower down, as outcroppings, so that they emerge as huge stone figures, higher than the walls they built. In both Norwegian and English, the pronoun that begins line 4 is intentionally ambiguous.

Stave Churches   *p. 93*
The poem takes as its starting point the distinctive wooden churches that were built in Norway (especially in the western parts of it) during the Middle Ages. The earliest surviving stave churches date from the first half of the twelfth century. The timber is often reddish brown; some of the exterior carved ornaments resemble wings or the figureheads of sailing ships.

Santa Maria, Pinta and Niña: I have corrected "Nina" to "Niña" in the Norwegian text.

Laudate: The verse is from Psalm 113: "Praise, O ye servants of the Lord, praise the name of the Lord."

Old Men's Graves   *p. 101*
Rolf Jacobsen gave me permission, when I was editing *TSA*, to restore wording that appears in this poem in editions earlier than *SD 1977*. He had agreed to change "menn" (men) to "folk" (people) in response to objections from certain feminists that the poem was not inclusive. (He wrote that he had wished to avoid having a "label" slapped on him in the event he refused.) Given that "ungdommens graver" (young people's graves) carries an unavoidable association with the graves of soldiers (who in Jacobsen's lifetime were almost exclusively male), the objections seem obtuse.

The Foundryman of Waterfalls   *p. 109*

The sound of a waterfall in a forest changes as one moves. Here Jacobsen imagines a mythical spirit of the waterfalls, who is responsible for their noise and their work.

Mirror Lakes   *p. 111*

Norwegian editions do not have a comma after stanza 3, line 2. Jacobsen inserted a comma after "yoghien" on the galley proofs of *TSA;* I therefore printed the comma in *TSA* and have retained it here.

In the Hall of Gobelin Tapestries   *p. 119*

By capitalizing *Timian* (third stanza), Jacobsen makes "thyme" a fictitious painter who is paired with Botticelli in an amusing, and untranslatable, pun on "Titian." *Kløverknekt* (fifth stanza), literally "clover-knave," also means the Knave (or Jack) of Clubs.

In the Norwegian text I have emended "Fransiscus" to "Franciscus." But I have retained Jacobsen's use of the German spelling "Ignazius," though this may have been an oversight (perhaps influenced by the ecclesiastical pronunciation of the Latin form "Ignatius," which is the usual spelling in Norwegian).

In January   *p. 125*

In the first edition of *Brev til lyset,* a page division falls after line 3 of the fifth stanza. As a result of this accidental division, *SD 1973* inserts a blank line at this point, thus dividing into two what Jacobsen intended to be a single stanza. (Jacobsen confirmed this intention in writing in May 1985; he also removed the spurious stanza break when he marked the galley proofs of *TSA.*) All subsequent editions of *Samlede dikt* (including *SD 1999*), as well as *AMD*, repeat the blank line. I removed it in *TSA* and have done so here as well.

The Memory of Horses   *p. 141*

The last line of the first stanza would seem to reverse the terms of the well-known Bible story in Genesis 41, in which Joseph interprets the Pharaoh's dream to mean that seven years of plenty will be followed by seven years of famine and counsels the Pharaoh to gather in and put aside one-fifth of the crop from each year of plenty. (The word *armoden* [poverty, want], however, occurs in the Norwegian Bible Society's 1930 translation of the Bible only in Proverbs 6 and 24.)

Glass Soldiers   *p. 149*

At the end of the translation, I have departed slightly from the literal sense of the last line of the Norwegian in order to convey more clearly the image that I believe is intended. As a result, I have also had to adjust the line breaks to avoid an overly long last line and to achieve an effect of balanced phrases equivalent to that found in the Norwegian.

The Towers in Bologna   *p. 151*

I have retained here the stanza break between stanzas 2 and 3 that appears in the first edition of *Brev til lyset.* This break is missing in *SD 1977, 1982,* and *1986,* as well as in *AMD,* no doubt because a page division coincided with it in *SD 1973.*

I have corrected the misspellings "Assinella," "Assinelli," and "Piazensa" that appear in various Norwegian editions.

The Catacombs of San Callisto   *p. 155*

In the first edition of *Brev til lyset,* each stanza of this poem consists of one long verse line. Various editions of *Samlede dikt* change this layout in various ways. In correspondence in May 1985, Jacobsen advised me to retain the original layout (but to incorporate later revisions to wording and punctuation). He also marked each stanza as one long line on the galley proofs of *TSA.*

Thoughts upon Listening In on a Radio Telescope   *p. 165*

The reference to the Sagene ['sä-ge-ne] trolley is a joke: Sagene is a section of Oslo just outside the downtown area; the trolley is an especially old one.

Unthinking—   *p. 167*

Rolf Jacobsen gave me permission, when I was editing *TSA,* to restore wording that appears in this poem in editions earlier than *SD 1977.* As in the case of "Gamle menns graver" ("Old Men's Graves"), he had agreed to make a change in response to objections from certain feminists: "kvinnenes små lykker" (women's small delights) was made to read "de aldrendes små lykker" (the small delights of the elderly—or should that be *senior citizens?*).

Waiting Time   *p. 173*

Oboslisten (the Oslo Housing list): *Obos* is an acronym for Oslo bolig- og sparelag, or Oslo Housing and Savings Company. The wait for an apartment can take many years.

Hush——   *p. 175*

I have followed *SD 1999* in inserting a period at the end of the first line.

Peasant Norway   *p. 177*

It is not clear how far back in time the poem goes. The feudal system in Norway was brought to an end in the course of the eighteenth century. By 1750 a majority of farmers owned their own land. The constitution of 1814 gave power to the farmers; the nobility was abolished in 1821. On the other hand, in 1850 there were still large numbers of *husmenn*, or cotters, who did not own the land they worked and had little political power. The cotters survived, in dwindling numbers, into the twentieth century.

Some   *p. 179*

Since *noen* means both "someone" and "some (people)," the changes in number are a matter of interpretation and move through the poem more sinuously in Norwegian than in English.

Signs of Winter   *p. 185*

Line 2 is a free rendering based on an explanation provided by Rolf Jacobsen: "the rotting leaves give off an odor of formaldehyde." The original means, literally, "The aspens' leaves are killed with formalin capsules."

This poem was deleted from *AMD*.

Angelus   *p. 197*

The title is the name of a devotion that commemorates the Annunciation; it is the first word of the versicle "Angelus domini nuntiavit Mariæ," "The angel of the Lord announced unto Mary" (Luke 1:28). The quotation at the end of the first stanza, well known as part of the Magnificat, is from Luke 1:48 (see Samuel 1:11 for the Old Testament analogue). The Norwegian text does not quote the passage with perfect accuracy; either Jacobsen was quoting from memory or he adjusted the wording slightly to suit his lines. By the time he wrote the poems in *Pass for dørene — dørene lukkes*, Jacobsen seems to have been using the spellings "meg, deg, seg" fairly consistently. However, in response to a question I sent him in May 1985 he agreed that the older spelling "mig" should be retained in the biblical quotation.

"Hva sier stjernene" ("What Do the Stars Say") is a common title for astrology columns in newspapers.

In stanza 1, line 9, the first edition of *Pass for dørene — dørene lukkes* has a comma after "sperma." *SD 1973, 1977, 1982,* and *1986,* as well as *AMD,* print a period instead. *SD 1999* restores the comma. Jacobsen confirmed that the comma is correct; he also marked the comma on the galley proofs of *TSA*. I have therefore retained it; but I have incorporated revisions to wording that appear in various editions of *Samlede dikt*.

Briefing   *p. 199*

The beginning of the poem refers to Matthew 19:14 and Mark 10:14.

All Norwegian editions have "Pst. alle små." in line 3. In response to questions I sent him on 26 December 1982, Jacobsen advised that this should be "Pst! Alle små." It happened that the galley proofs of *TSA* incorrectly set a question mark after "Pst"; Jacobsen corrected it to an exclamation point.

Epilogue   *p. 201*

"Aurora" in the subtitle refers only to the dawn, not to northern lights. The painter and graphic artist Anne-Lise Knoff (born in Hamar in 1937) became a steadfast friend of Jacobsen's; she provided illustrations for *AMD*.

SD 1977, 1982, and *1986,* as well as *AMD,* combine the last two lines of the first stanza into a single long line and eliminate the stanza break. I have not incorporated these changes, preferring to follow the first edition of *Pass for dørene — dørene lukkes* and *SD 1973,* which is in general far more reliable typographically than all subsequent editions of Jacobsen's work until *SD 1999.*

All Norwegian editions use the spelling "Arkturus," which has never been an accepted spelling. Jacobsen wrote "Arcturus" in "Katakombene i San Callisto" ("The Catacombs of San Callisto"), and in the present poem he corrected the *k* to a *c* on the galley proofs of *TSA.* In the last line I have emended "trotsige" (a Swedish spelling) to "trossige."

Avaldsnes   *p. 211*

Avaldsnes ['ä-väls-ˌneʸs] is a point, or headland, on the west coast of Norway, just south of Haugesund, on the eastern shore of the island of Karmøy.

Yggdrasil [*Norw.* 'ʊeg-drä-ˌsēl, *Engl.* 'ig-drə-ˌsil]: in Norse mythology, the tree of the universe, a huge ash tree that binds heaven, earth, and hell together.

Old Cities in Auvergne   *p. 213*

Norwegian distinguishes between *småbyer,* which corresponds to American "small towns," and *små byer,* which indicates population centers that are small but not necessarily insignificant or provincial. I chose to use "cities" rather than "towns" to indicate the self-containment and importance of the centers described here, and chose "old" rather than "small" as a way of suggesting both their smallness (since very large cities are relatively recent phenomena) and the salient characteristic that emerges from the poem.

On the galley proofs of *TSA,* Jacobsen inserted a comma after the penultimate line of the first stanza. I have corrected "Puy-de-Dome" to "Puy-de-Dôme" in the Norwegian text.

Hallingskeid   *p. 217*

Hallingskeid ['hä-liŋ-ˌshʸaēd] is a railroad station on the Bergen line, between Finse and Myrdal, on the Hardanger Plateau. There are many short tunnels and snow shelters between Finse and Myrdal; west of Myrdal the line passes through the Gravahals Tunnel, which is almost 3 miles (5 km) long. This part of the line joins the eastern and western parts of the country, which have distinct landscapes and even different traditional styles of house construction.

Reinunga ['raēn-ˌuŋ-ä] is the name of a valley, a lake, and a tunnel just east of Myrdal station. Såta ['sȯ-tä] is a mountain in the same area.

Sneoverbygget (snow shelter): a roofed structure, partly open on the downhill side, built over railway tracks that run along a slope where avalanches are likely to occur.

Blind Words   *p. 221*

Norwegian editions print "for lysene er brent ned" in line 4. The galley proofs of *TSA* contain a correction of *for* to *før* in my hand, apparently made after consultation with Jacobsen by telephone. I have retained *før* here, but it seems likely that Jacobsen originally wrote *for;* if *for* had been a typographical error, I doubt he would have missed it in reading proofs of *SD 1973* and *1977.* (*SD 1982* had so many errors that any given one might well have slipped by; and Jacobsen was not given the opportunity to make changes or corrections to *SD 1986,* except in the section containing the poems from *Nattåpent.*)

We Who Live near the Railway   *p. 233*

The Dovre ['dòv-re] Mountains are a region of high mountains that spans the boundaries of four counties. Dovre is a railroad station in the Valley of Gudbrandsdal, just south of Dombås on the line to Trondheim, about 125 miles (200 km) northwest of Hamar. (For Gudbrandsdalen ['gūed-bräns-ˌdäl-ᵊn], see the note to "In the Varald Forest.")

Fokkstu ['fók-ˌstūē] is the first railroad station north of Dombås; the bogs lie in the surrounding area. Hjerkinn ['yar-kin] is the third railroad station north of Dombås. The dome is an elevated area north and east of the station; it marks the highest point on the old "King's Highway" over the Dovre Mountains.

For *boggi,* see the note to "Railroad Country."

Rolf Jacobsen gave me permission, when I was editing *TSA,* to restore wording that appears in this poem in editions earlier than *SD 1982.* As in "Gamle menns graver" ("Old Men's Graves") and "Tankeløs—" ("Unthinking—"), he had agreed to make a change in response to objections from certain feminists: "Kvinneår" (Women's Year) was made to read "Barneår" (Year of the Child); these refer to years of special attention to women's and children's issues, declared by the United Nations.

Jacobsen confirmed in writing in May 1985 that "inn i" in stanza 1, line 8 of the Norwegian text should read "inni"; he also marked the change on the galley proofs of *TSA.*

Fasten Your Seat Belts—   *p. 239*

In the Norwegian title and in the last stanza, I have corrected the solid spelling "seatbelts" that Jacobsen used. Italic font in the translation marks phrases that are in English in the Norwegian text.

The Media Poem   *p. 245*

Lake Mjøsa ['myōē-sä] is the largest lake in Norway; Hamar is situated on its eastern shore.

In response to questions I sent him on 26 December 1982, Jacobsen confirmed that there should be a period at the end of stanza 1, line 3 (this was omitted in Norwegian editions).

In stanza 2 I have for once incorporated changes that appear for the first time in *AMD:* the use of uppercase letters for the last phrase in line 3; the change from "ett" to "et" in line 4; and the correction of "i allfall" to "iallfall" in line 6.

Look Up (N.B. N.B.)   *p. 251*

Ullernåsen ['ül-ern-ˌòs-ᵊn] is an affluent suburb west of Oslo.
This poem was deleted from *AMD.*

To You   *p. 259*

In stanza 3, line 1, I have incorporated the change from "enda" to "ennå" that appears in *AMD*, because I am persuaded that by the time he wrote the poems in *Tenk på noe annet,* Jacobsen was using "ennå" fairly consistently as the adverb of time that corresponds to English "still." Note, however, that he still used "enda" as the adverb of degree: see stanza 4, line 2 in this poem, for example.

Beyond Grorud—   *p. 263*

Olav H. Hauge (1907–1994), a contemporary of Jacobsen, is considered one of the great Norwegian poets of the twentieth century.

Grorud ['grü-ˌrᵫd] is a "satellite town" east of Oslo. Hakadal ['hä-kä-ˌdäl] is a town and railroad station about 12 miles (20 km) north of Oslo. Sokna ['sòk-nä] is a town and railroad station on the Bergen line, about 40 miles (60 km) northwest of Oslo.

Hundvåko   *p. 265*

Hundvåko ['hún-ˌvò-kü] is an island off the west coast of Norway, south of Bergen; Hangur ['häŋ-ˌᵫr] is one of the mountains near the town of Voss, northwest of Bergen.

Skriulaupen ['skrē-yü-ˌlaᵘp-ᵊn], Framrusthovdi ['främ-rùst-ˌhòv-dē], and Uppnostindann' ['üp-nòs-ˌtin-dän] are all mountains in Oppland County.

Tindulvstølane ['tin-dùl-ˌstœ-lä-ne]: "Støl" denotes a mountain pasture where cattle are taken to graze in the summertime ("stølane" is the definite plural form in Nynorsk). There is no record of a real place called Tindulvstølane. Either this was a name in local use that did not get recorded (probably in Nord Aurdal, a township in Oppland County, where there is a lake called Tindulvtjernet), or Jacobsen invented it, though it is also possible that he remembered a real name incorrectly. (Thanks to Tom Schmidt of the University of Oslo for his research on this place name.)

—More Mountains   *p. 269*

Norway has had three kings named Harald ['hä-räl] before the present one. The sense of the poem suggests that the king referred to here is Harald Hårfager

("Fairhair"), whom tradition credits with having founded a united Norway in 872 A.D.

The Bells from Assisi   *p. 271*
Assisi stands on a high plateau; when birds fly out from it they are immediately far above the surrounding plains. So "high against the heavens" is a precise image.

"Silvery Moon"   *p. 273*
The title derives from the pop song "By the Light of the Silvery Moon," by Ray Noble and Snookie Lanson.

Italic font in the translation marks phrases that are in English in the Norwegian text.

Kersey Coates is a section of Jackson, which is the part of Kansas City, Missouri, that lies immediately to the southeast of the confluence of the two rivers.

The phrase "full og fager" at the end of the poem corresponds to "full and fair," but contains a pun, since *full* also means "drunk."

In the first edition of *Tenk på noe annet*, a stanza break appears to coincide with a page division after line 11 of the third stanza. In correspondence in May 1985, Jacobsen advised that a break was not necessary there. I have ignored a stanza break that appears in *AMD* (between lines 7 and 8 of stanza 5), because I believe it is spurious and arises from a page division that falls in this place in *SD 1986*. Jacobsen approved galley proofs of *TSA* on which this poem has five stanzas.

The Inland Line   *p. 277*
The Inland Line is the name of the entire rail line that runs down the center of Sweden from Gällivare in the north to Kristinehamn in the south (a distance of 780 miles, or 1,290 km). The poem traces a trip south to Östersund. (North of Gällivare a connecting line continues to Narvik, on the northwest coast of Norway.)

The state built the part of the line that was hardest to build (from Gällivare to Steg, 575 miles, or 930 km) between 1907 and 1937. The more southerly stretches were built much earlier in various stages by private companies and later taken over by the state. The main purpose of these early lines was to carry ore. By 1900, however, the Swedish General Staff had realized that an extended and unified railway in the area would contribute significantly to the defense of northern Sweden. But the Inland Line did not prosper as was hoped.

Gällivare ['ye-li-‚vä-re] lies only 4 miles (6 km) south of Malmberget ("Ore Mountain"). It has been a center for mining in the area since the 1870s. Östersund [‚œs-ter-'sünd], a city in central Sweden, was founded in the 1780s, developed slowly, and had only five hundred inhabitants by 1850. The railroad arrived in 1882. In 1893 the Norrlands Artillery Regiment was garrisoned there; it was joined within twenty years by two other regiments.

Kåbdalis ['kòb-‚dä-lis]; Moskosel ['müs-kü-‚sel]; Koosakåbbå ['kü-sä-'kò-bò], also spelled Kuosakåbbå; and Vargtandberget ['väry-ˌtän-'bar-yet], also called Järvtandberget, are stations on the Inland Line, south of Gällivare. The poem's prophecy was fulfilled: by 1984 the last-named station had vanished from the map.

Vojmån ['vȯi-mȯn] is a railroad station two-thirds of the way from Gällivare to Östersund. The Lule ['lü-le], the Pite ['pē-te], and the Ume ['ü-me] are three large rivers in northern Sweden that flow from northwest to southeast across the entire breadth of the country and empty into the Gulf of Bothnia.

Ulriksfors [ˌül-riks-'fȯsh] is a town and railroad station about 55 miles (90 km) northeast of Östersund.

Jacobsen advised me (May 1985) to insert a comma after the word *krig* in the penultimate line of this poem. He also marked the comma on the galley proofs of *TSA*.

Trees in Autumn   *p. 283*

In the last line of the Norwegian text I have retained the spelling "gjennem-" because it seems possible that the final word, *dem*, led Jacobsen to prefer this older form to the newer "gjennom" that he used in all other instances in his last three books.

Thoughts at Lake Sjodal   *p. 285*

Lake Sjodal ['shü-ˌdäl]: a lake in two parts (Upper and Lower) formed by a widening of the Sjoa River, which runs in the Valley of Sjodal from Gjende (see below) into the Gudbrandsdal river basin.

Hávamál ['hä-vä-ˌmäl]: one of the best-known poems in the Poetic Edda; its title means "Sayings of the High One" (i.e., Odin).

Gjende Rapids: Gjende ['yen-de] is the name of a lake in Oppland County; *Gjendeoset* refers to the outlet of the lake, where the water flows with some speed. In order to convey this, I've taken the liberty of using *rapids* (a word that usually suggests a river).

I have ignored a stanza break in *AMD* (between lines 3 and 4 of stanza 2), because I believe it is spurious and arises from a page division that falls in this place in *SD 1986*.

Suddenly. In December   *p. 287*

I have referred to the text published in *Poesi Magasin*, No. 2 (1984), p. 3, to restore a line in stanza 4 that has been deleted or omitted in *Nattåpent* and *AMD*; but in other respects I have reproduced the Norwegian text of this poem as it appears in these two books.

This poem begins a suite of poems from the book *Nattåpent* (Night Watch) that deals with the death of Jacobsen's wife, Petra, and his memories of their marriage. Petra Tendø was born in 1912. She and Rolf Jacobsen probably met in late 1937 or early 1938; they were married on 21 December 1940 (see the poem "Barbed-wire Winter"), and she took his surname. She died on 2 December 1983.

Barbed-wire Winter   *p. 291*

I have ignored a change in *AMD* that makes line 9 begin with an uppercase *N*. I believe the lowercase *n* in the first edition of *Nattåpent* was both intentional and correct, since line 9 is spoken by the same person who speaks line 8 and the two lines can be taken as a single sentence. An uppercase *N* would suggest that a second speaker was replying to the first. It seems likely that the period at the end of line 8 in Norwegian editions is a typographical error and that a comma was intended, so I have made the emendation here.

A Poem on the River Glåma   *p. 303*

This is the last poem that Rolf Jacobsen published during his lifetime.

Glåma ['glö-mä]: The name of the river is usually spelled "Glomma"; Jacobsen here uses a dialectical form. The River Glomma is the largest river in Norway and one of the largest in northern Europe. It is over 360 miles (600 km) long and flows mainly southward, from Lake Aursunden, north of Røros, to Fredrikstad, where it empties into the Oslo Fjord. For many years it was used for floating timber.

Solør ['sü-ˌlœr]: a region in the southern part of Hedmark County that straddles the Glomma; the eastern part of it includes Finnskogene and borders on Sweden. In 1913, when Rolf Jacobsen was a boy of six, his family moved from Oslo (then Kristiania) to Flisa, the largest village in the municipal district of Åsnes, which lies in Solør. Jacobsen spent his boyhood here (until 1920, when he was thirteen and was shipped back to Kristiania to attend school there); he returned in 1934, and in 1937 he took charge of the Flisa office of the daily newspaper *Kongsvinger Arbeiderblad*, the largest paper in the region. He held this position until early 1941, when he was made editor of *Kongsvinger Arbeiderblad* and moved to Kongsvinger. Thus he had long-standing and varied connections to the Solør region.

Lauta ['laüʸ-tä]: a small hamlet on the west side of the Glomma, near Flisa.

Index of Titles

Note: The Norwegian alphabet has three more letters than the English one: æ, ø, and å follow z in that order and are treated here as in Norwegian.

Index of First Lines

Note: The Norwegian alphabet has three more letters than the English one: æ, ø, and å follow z in that order and are treated here as in Norwegian.